AF391710

———————

Mondrala Press wishes to thank all its friends, fans, patrons, and investors for making this book possible, and especially:

Ms. Randa Dumanian
Mr. and Mrs. Karol and Dagmara Maziukiewicz
de domo Sowul

without whose enthusiasm and open hearts this book could never have happened.

———————

ABOUT THE AUTHOR

Aleksander Krawczuk (1922-2023) was a noted scholar of Greek and Roman antiquity, a professor at the Jagiellonian University, a former minister of culture, and an author of over 30 popular and widely translated books on the subject of the Antique. For fifty years, his books have enjoyed great popularity among a whole army of devoted fans—many of them people who had never taken interest in the Antique until they picked up one of his books.

What other scholar of antiquity writes popular best-sellers? Yet, at one point, the good professor even hosted an internationally syndicated TV program on ancient Greece and Rome. Alas, due to Russian cultural policies during the Cold War, it was very difficult to publish Polish books in the West. The current effort tries to work off the backlog.

This book appears as part of a project to translate all of the works of Aleksander Krawczuk into English. The following titles have appeared already:

Seven Against Thebes: Myth and History
A Meeting in Oea, or Concerning Plato
The Last Olympiad: Twilight of Antiquity
Titus and Berenice: Jews, Romans, War, and a Legendary Love Story
Rome and Jerusalem
The Thirteenth Apostle: Constantine the Great
The Devil's Brood: the Sons of Constantine

Five more titles will appear in 2025:

Julian the Apostate
Pericles and Apamea
The Case of Alcibiades, or, Ambition
The Tombs of Chaeronea, or, Concerning the Fall of Greece
Conversations with Petronius

Follow the series here: https://www.amazon.com/dp/B0BHF7KVTK

TRANSLATOR'S SPECIAL REQUEST
Translating and publishing this series of books has been a labor of
love for me. I grew up reading it, and I have always wanted to be able
to share it with my American friends. And finally, here it is.
It will not make me rich, but if you liked the book, would you please
recommend it to a friend?
And if you could give it an Amazon review,
you will be helping others find it!
https://www.amazon.com/dp/B0D2V3TVL4

THANK YOU!

THE THIRTEENTH APOSTLE

CONSTANTINE THE GREAT

by Aleksander Krawczuk
translated by Tom Pinch

MONDRALA PRESS

Illustrations.
1. *The Trophy of Constantine, with Victory at left crowning the emperor with a laurel, behind them a bounty of arms, armor, prisoners, and Maxentius' head on a stick.* After Rubens, Draftsman and Engraver unknown, published in Paris by Balthazar Montcornet, circa 1650. (source: Metropolitian Museum of Art, New York).
2. *A. Constantinus in Anglia natus ibiq. Imperator creatus.* Drawn by Nicolò Circignani, engraved by Giovani Battista de Cavalieri, published by Giovanni Antonio de Paoli in Rome, about 1620. (Collection Acc. Dei Lincei)
3. *The council of Nicea..* Drawn and engraved by unown, published in London 1683 for Richard Chistvel.
4. *St. Helen discovers the True Cross.* Drawn by Nicolò Circignani , engraved by Giovani Battista de Cavalieri, published by Giovanni Antonio de Paoli in Rome, about 1620. (Collection Acc. Dei Lincei)
Back cover: *Constatine's Dream*, part of the fresco cycle by Piero della Francesca in the Basilica of Saint Francis in Arezzo.

Aleksander Krawczuk
THE CHRISTIAN TRILOGY

The Thirteenth Apostle: Constantine the Great
The Devil's Brood: The Sons of Constantine
Julian the Apostate

TABLE OF CONTENTS

Part One
DIOCLETIAN 15

**Part Two
FROM YORK TO ROME 77**

**Part Three
FROM MILAN TO NICAEA 137**

Part One
DIOCLETIAN

Flavius Vopiscus:
From Ctesiphon to Nicomedia

In AD 283, Emperor Carus set out against the Persians with his younger son, Numerian. He easily took Mesopotamia and reached Ctesiphon, a city on the eastern bank of the Tigris. The Persians, absorbed in internal disputes, did not put up much resistance. Carus thus earned the title *Persicus Maximus*: the greatest victor over the Persians. But, at the urging of his Praetorian Prefect, Aper (who wanted to destroy the emperor in order to seize power himself), he went too far too fast.

Some claim that Carus died of a disease. But most maintain that he was struck by lightning. And it cannot be denied that at the moment of his death, there was a thunder strike. The noise was so terrifying that many died out of fear. Or that's what people said, anyhow.

Julius Calpurnius, the head of the imperial secretariat, sent a letter to the prefect of Rome regarding the circumstances of Carus's death. He wrote in it, among other things:

> When Carus, our beloved emperor, was sick and lying bedridden in his tent, suddenly, a great storm arose, and the world was plunged into such darkness that we could not see one other. In the unceasing

strikes of lightning that followed, we lost all sense of place and time. Suddenly, there was a cry: "The Emperor is dead!" And this happened after an especially loud thunderclap, which terrified everyone. And then the emperor's attendants, grieving over the death of their master, set his tent on fire. Hence, the rumor arose that his death was caused by lighting, but as far as we know, the cause of his death was an illness.

I quote this letter because many say:

> Surely, there is a Divine prohibition that no Roman emperor may go further east than Ctesiphon and live. Carus was killed by lightning because he dared to cross that boundary.

But let us leave such base arguments to cowards; the courageous shall surely trample them underfoot! For it is certain that the Persians can be defeated and the Ctesiphon line exceeded. Our most sacred Caesar Galerius has proven this beyond all doubt. If only we may not lose the current favor of the gods!

After his father's death, Numerian decided to end the war and led the army back home. But because he suffered from an inflammation of the eyes—a chronic condition he had acquired by working late into the night—he traveled in a closed litter. And at that point, the perfidious Praetorian Prefect Aper (who was Numerian's father-in-law) murdered him treacherously. For many days thereafter, the soldiers inquired about the emperor's health, but Aper always answered them:

"The emperor does not appear in public because his eyes hurt from the wind and the sun."

Only when the army reached Nicomedia did the stench of the decaying corpse reveal the crime. The soldiers attacked Aper. They dragged him into the main square of the camp and stood him in the main square next to the standards. Masses of soldiers gathered, and in the blink of an eye, a podium was erected. The men were trying to choose someone who could best avenge Numerian's death and rule the empire in his place. And, by divine inspiration, Diocletian was unanimously acclaimed emperor.

He was then the commander of the imperial bodyguard. It is said that many signs had predicted that he would reign one day. He was a fine man, clever, devoted to the nation, loyal to his friends, and always ready to face bravely all challenges of life. His actions were always prudent, and even if he sometimes acted ruthlessly, he generally suppressed the wilder impulses of his heart.

When he ascended the podium to accept the title of Augustus, the men demanded to know how Numerian died. At this, Diocletian drew his sword and, with one blow, cut Aper down, shouting:

"Here is the murderer of the emperor!"

Many years later, my grandfather told me that he had been present at this rally and that Diocletian then added these words:

> You can be proud, Aper!
> The hand of Aeneas has struck you!

This last sentence comes from Virgil's Aeneid. A literary quotation may seem unusual coming from the lips of a soldier. But I happen to know that many military men can skillfully quote dramatists and poets, both Greek and Roman.

My grandfather also told me what he had heard the following story from Diocletian himself:

At one time, he served in Gaul, in the country of the Tungres,[1] as a low-ranking officer. Staying at an inn somewhere, paying his bill, and omitting the tip, he was told by his landlady, who was a druidic priestess:

"You are too cheap, Diocletian!"

He joked:

"When I am emperor, I will be generous!"

But to this, she replied:

"You will become emperor only after you kill a boar."

Diocletian, a secretive man by nature, smiled at this and did not respond. But from then on, whenever the opportunity presented

---

[1] *Civitas Tungrorum* was a large Roman administrative district in today's eastern Belgium and the southern Netherlands.

itself on a hunt, he always killed the boar with his own hand. Meanwhile, first Aurelian became emperor, then Probus, then Tacitus, and finally Carus. Diocletian said:

"I keep killing boars, but others eat the meat!"

And it is common knowledge that when he killed Aper, he sighed:

"Finally, I got the right boar!"

(In Latin, *aper* means a boar).

My grandfather related to me also the following words of Diocletian:

"I had no other reason to kill him with my own hand except to fulfill the prophecy of the druidess. I certainly did not wish to appear violent or unpredictable, certainly not at the outset of my reign. But I killed him because Fate had willed it."[2]

Has There Been a Flavius Vopiscus?

The previous chapter is based on the narrative of a certain Flavius Vopiscus. It is not, however, a translation of the Latin text but rather a loose paraphrase. In order to make the course of events easier to follow, several details from other sources[3] have been added, and some explanations introduced into the text.

Who was this Vopiscus, whose grandfather was said to have participated in the events at Nicomedia and knew Diocletian personally? The answer is not simple.

In the fourth century AD, a Latin work called *Scriptores Historiae Augustae* ("Writers of Imperial History") appeared. It contains the biographies of Roman emperors from Hadrian to Numerian, i.e., from AD 117 to 284, although with some gaps. The book is allegedly the collective work of six authors. We say "allegedly" because certain evidence suggests that, in fact, there was only one

---

[2] Scriptores Historiae Augustae, Carus, 8-9; 12-15

[3] Aurelius Victor, *De Caesaribus,* 38-39; Eutropius, IX 10

author who—for unknown reasons—took on six different names. Flavius Vopiscus is listed as the author of the last part of the collection, covering the reigns of emperors from Aurelian to Numerian.

If the book really had a single author, it would be a truly elaborate hoax. But the work itself is also unusual: there are many fabrications and distortions in it, as well as many anachronisms. It seems that it was created mainly to smuggle allusions to some current affairs under the guise of a historical account of an ancient past. However, it is difficult to determine what events and people these allusions referred to because, despite many studies, it has not been possible to determine the date of writing of this collection of lives.

The author (or authors) tries to give the impression that he is writing during his reign of Diocletian or Constantine and, therefore, in the first decades of the fourth century, which is obviously false. In fact, the work was written after the reign of Julian the Apostate (AD 361–363) and almost certainly at the end of the fourth century.

This does not mean, however, that everything in the account should be considered worthless or fictitious. The author undoubtedly relied on solid material, which he freely adapted to his needs. His reports should neither be accepted as they stand nor rejected out of hand, but in every case, examined and confronted with other sources. The man named Flavius Vopiscus probably did not exist at all, but the story told under his name may be largely true.

The Cursed Third Century

The mysterious death of one emperor during a foreign war; the equally mysterious murder of his son; and the killing of the Praetorian Prefect in front of the whole army—all this might seem an invention of a highly imaginative mind of a novelist. And yet, the essential outline of the story presented by Flavius Vopiscus seems credible: other sources, though passing and cursory, seem to confirm this account. Of course, some details of the story appear to discredit themselves by their sheer improbability, but we should not be too hasty to judge: surely, Vopiscus's contemporaries looked at the events of the year 284 as something almost normal: they were entirely consistent with the experience of the preceding two generations.

Almost exactly fifty years earlier, in 235, emperor Alexander Severus died at the hands of his soldiers. From then on, the Empire saw a bloody *coup d'etat* practically every other year. Within half a century, twenty-two emperors occupied the throne, and that's not counting those flash-in-the-pans who never gained control of the whole empire. Almost all were elevated to the purple by the army, and with very few exceptions, nearly all died a violent death. The killers were almost always their own soldiers or power-hungry individuals from their immediate surroundings. Only six emperors died on the battlefield.

From within, the Empire was convulsed by wars for the throne, revolts of governors, attempts by provinces to break away, and uprisings of the oppressed population. From the outside, hordes of barbarians, especially Germans, invaded the borders. Alemanni crossed the Danube and the upper Rhine and devastated Gaul, the Alpine countries, and northern Italy. Franks crossed the lower Rhine and reached as far as Galicia in Spain. Goths from the shores of the Black Sea and their allies crossed the Danube but also came by sea: they ravaged the provinces of the Balkan peninsula and Asia Minor. And in the east, across the Euphrates, a great military power arose: the Sassanid monarchy—the Romans simply called them Persians. Because the Sassanids claimed all the lands of the Middle East as part of the ancient Achaemenid inheritance, bloody struggles with them became practically incessant, and their course was rarely as successful for the Romans as during the reign of Carus, who managed to reach as far as Ctesiphon.

While wars ravaged the economy and laid waste the countryside, the tax burden on the civilian population rose sharply because of the enormous cost of maintaining the army. State bureaucracy expanded vastly to exact the heavy tolls even while fields turned fallow, cities fell into decline, trade dwindled, and life became brutish and short. The treasury, deprived of reserves, resorted to suicidal means, time and again adulterating money, without realizing—or perhaps realizing fully—that for the sake of meeting short-term needs, it caused irreparable long-term damage to the economy.

There was a shortage of labor. The land was cultivated mainly by the *coloni*—small tenant farmers—personally free, but in essence not much better off than slaves; and, absent victorious wars of conquest, the supply of slaves had collapsed. The lower classes, the so-called *humiliores*, were ruthlessly exploited by the upper classes, the *honestiores*, and the state treated both with equal brutality.

And thus, the empire experienced a deep and long-lasting crisis in the third century. We would seek in vain for the mainsprings of this phenomenon because many factors—economic, social, climatic, and military—overlapped and interconnected, but the consequences were disastrous. The empire stood over an abyss. It seemed that nothing could arrest the endless procession of murders, wars, and disasters. Diocletian's murder of Aper seemed just one more. And yet, the reader can sense that Flavius Vopiscus is favorably disposed to the new emperor. He says that he was acclaimed emperor by "Divine inspiration;" that his future greatness had been predicted by prophetic signs, and that he killed Aper only to fulfill the prophecy of a druidess.

So who was this Diocletian? What paths had taken him to the podium in the camp in Nicomedia? And why did the historian like him?

Diocletian's Career

Like most emperors of the third century, the murderer of Aper had come from humble origins. He was born in Dalmatia—today's Croatia, probably near Salona, today's Solin, maybe even near the town where he later built a grand palace—in today's Split. He was born about AD 240, meaning that he was just over forty when he took power in 284.

His contemporaries knew little about his descent, and his parents were never mentioned. Some claimed that Diocletian's father had been a minor bureaucrat: the Roman administration employed whole armies of badly paid scribes. Others maintained that the future emperor had once worked as a freedman of a certain senator—and, therefore, was the son of slaves. This last version seems unlikely.[4]

Prior to his acclamation, his name had been Gaius Valerius Diocles. The name seems to suggest that an ancestor of his had been a Greek slave named Diocles and was freed by some Valerius. As emperor, he took the name Gaius Aurelius Valerius Diocletianus: Aurelius because several emperors had born that name, and the ending *-tianus* because it made the whole thing sound more dignified and more Roman.

Diocles had entered military service as a young man. He must have distinguished himself with exceptional courage and energy, for he quickly rose through the ranks to the high position of the commander of the emperor's bodyguard.

Our historian, Vopiscus, describes the course of events between Ctesiphon and Nicomedia in a way which portrays the new ruler's first action as an act of just punishment. However, we are entitled to some doubts.

First off, the circumstances of Carus's death, like those of Numerian's, seem suspicious, to say the least. And if both emperors had been murdered, how could Aper, the Praetorian Prefect, have murdered them without the knowledge—perhaps even assistance—of the commander of the bodyguard, Diocles? Perhaps the two had conspired in the murders? If so, did the bolder of the two decide to eliminate the other and accuse him of being the murderer?

Or perhaps Numerian died a natural death after all? Perhaps Aper only kept it secret, hoping to deliver the army safely to the rightful heir to the throne? This was Carinus, the elder son of Carus, and was in Italy. If so, Aper's loyalty ended up costing him his life: the revelation that Numerian was dead and that his death had been kept a

---

[4] Eutropius, IX, 19

secret gave rise to the suspicion that Aper had murdered Numerian. Who knows, perhaps the accusation was brought by Diocles?

Next: who acclaimed Diocles emperor? Our primary source, Vopiscus, says that Diocles was acclaimed "generally," "unanimously," and by "divine inspiration." Another account, although very brief, claims that Diocles was proposed by "his fellow officers."[5] This gives rise to the suspicion that there had been a wider conspiracy within the Army of the East directed against both Numerian and his father-in-law, Aper.

Further, contrary to what Vopiscus says, Diocletian never claimed to be the avenger of Numerian. On the contrary, he did his best to erase his predecessor's memory. Proof positive of this are inscriptions from which the names of Numerian and his brother Carinus were carefully erased—clearly on official orders. In fact, Diocletian later claimed that he had agreed to take imperial purple only to put an end to a bloody tyranny.

Many questions surround Diocletian's elevation to the throne.

The new emperor was acclaimed in the military camp near Nicomedia on September 17 or 18, AD 284. His subjects and his soldiers probably expected that his reign would be as brief as that of all the emperors of the last half a century—especially since a civil war was imminent, one with the West, which remained under the control of Carinus.

But things turned out differently. Diocletian defeated Carinus, although the victory did not come easily. A bloody battle in the summer of 285, fought near the confluence of the Morava and the Danube, near today's Bratislava, went against Diocletian. However, Carinus was then murdered by his own people on account of his "debauchery and cruelty." Or so our sources say.

From that point on, Diocletian reigned for twenty years, longer than any emperor in almost half a century. This alone must be

---

⁵ Aurelius Victor, *De Caesaribus*, 39, 1

considered a significant accomplishment. What is even more extraordinary, at the end of those twenty years, Diocletian retired of his own free will and lived out the rest of his life as a highly respected senior statesman, apparently devoted exclusively to growing vegetables in the gardens of his Dalmatian palace. In the entire history of the Roman Empire, this had never happened. Nor was it ever going to happen again.

What gave Rome such lasting political stability after such a long period of constant wars and upheavals? What was Diocletian's long rule like, and what impact did it have on the Empire?

In trying to understand the age of Diocletian, we will first turn to a contemporary of the events, the historian Lactantius. His figure will emerge gradually as we become acquainted with his texts. For now, it is enough to say that he was a professor of Latin rhetoric at the university of Nicomedia, that he owed his position to Diocletian but did not repay him for his appointment with the gratitude we might expect, and that he published his work mainly to slander that emperor, his co-rulers and successors. The work is titled *De mortibus persecutorum* ("On the deaths of our persecutors"). It is a political pamphlet written with undisguised bias. And while hate distorts the picture it presents, it is vivid and colorful even after the passage of centuries, and its passionate words of condemnation are perhaps the best place to start.

Lactantius:
A Portrait of the Emperor

Diocletian, the fount of criminal ideas and the cause of all misfortunes, the destroyer of everything, did not even keep his hands off God. He brought destruction upon the earth, both through his greed and his fear. First, he made three other men partners in his government. He divided the world into four parts, each with its own emperor, with the result that the standing armies multiplied because each of the four wanted to have more troops than the previous emperors who had ruled alone. And thus, the number of those to be fed so much exceeded the number of those feeding that the burden exhausted the means of the *coloni*; they fled the land, and their fields turned into wilderness.

To make state control ubiquitous, he divided the provinces into smaller units and appointed a multitude of governors and officials to each, even to cities: a multitude of financial officers, agents of government agencies, and deputy prefects. These men rarely attended to urgent civil matters, but they all gladly sentenced, confiscated, and outlawed. They imposed heavy obligations on the population, not often, but constantly. And in the process, they committed outrageous abuses. It became especially difficult to endure all the burdens associated with the conscription of soldiers.

The same Diocletian, driven by insatiable greed, never allowed his treasury to be depleted. He kept accumulating coin and created untouchable reserves. And when his harmful actions led to an enormous rise in prices, he tried to impose maximum prices for all goods by law. Little things without value became the cause of murder so that, out of fear, goods disappeared from the market altogether. Inflation raged on until life finally forced a repeal of the artificial prices, but not before they brought ruin to many.

Diocletian was also consumed by a boundless desire to build. Therefore, he put the provinces under tremendous pressure to provide workers, craftsmen, carts, and materials. He built basilicas here. A circus there. A mint over here. An armory there. A house for the wife here, there one for the daughter. Out of the blue, he demolished a large section of the city and drove off the people along with their wives and children as if they were fleeing invading barbarians. And when the work was completed at the cost of ruining many, the emperor declared:

"This is badly done. Redo it!"

So, he raged and overthrew everything once again. He went on and on. He wanted his Nicomedia to be equal to Rome.

I have not even mentioned that many people were murdered just so that their wealth could be confiscated: confiscation had been a frequent and common practice under previous emperors, but it was peculiar to Diocletian that whenever he saw a piece of better-cultivated land or a more ornate building, the owner was immediately brought to "justice" and accused of a crime punishable by death as if the emperor were unable to seize property without shedding blood![6]

The Tetrarchy

Reading the above, one might get the impression that Diocletian's reign was only a continuation of the instability that had scourged the empire for half a century. Yet, this would fly in the face of one fact: Diocletian stayed in power for over twenty years—until AD 305. He then laid down the imperial purple voluntarily and died a natural death in retirement. This suggests that matters stood somewhat differently from the way Lactantius paints them. The picture is certainly complex: Diocletian's measures were indeed harsh but were accepted by the inhabitants of the Empire.

Lactantius brings Diocletian's appointment of three co-regents to the forefront of his accusations, so let us deal with that matter first.

The formulation given by Lactantius: "he divided the world into four parts" is not really true. Although Diocletian did introduce a system of quadruple reign, which we usually refer to by the Greek term *tetrarchy*, the system arose gradually, and there was never any question of a division of the Empire.

In 286, Diocletian raised Maximian to the rank of Augustus. And while Maximian bore the same title as Diocletian, he could not compete with his colleague in authority—neither in theory nor in practice. This was clearly spelled out in the nicknames the two added

---

[6] Lactantius, VII

to their surnames. Diocletian's was *Iovius*, or Jovian, after the supreme deity of Rome, Jupiter, while Maximian received the name *Herculius*, i.e., Herculean. Absolutely everybody knew that Hercules was the *son* of Jupiter, and only thanks to his heroic deeds gained his father's *permission* to ascend to Mount Olympus.

In 293, the two Augustuses adopted younger colleagues and called them "Caesars." Diocletian appointed Galerius, while Maximian elevated Constantius. The former was nicknamed *Iovius*, after his Augustus; the latter—*Herculius,* after his. Even then, strictly speaking, one could at most talk about a division of the Empire into two competencies—eastern and western, with the Jovian pair ruling in the East and the Herculean pair—in the West. Only the Augustuses were entitled to dictate policy and promulgate laws—which they did jointly—while their Caesars limited themselves to their enforcement. The Caesars' task was to defend the borders.

Yes, certain spheres of influence were designated to facilitate administration: Diocletian dealt principally with the affairs of Asia Minor, Syria, Palestine, and Egypt; his Caesar—Galerius—watched over the Balkan provinces with their constantly threatened Danubian border; Maximian controlled Italy, Spain, and northern Africa, and Constantius controlled Britain and Gaul, with their Pictish and Germanic borders. Despite this, the Empire remained united, with the three "minor" emperors recognizing Diocletian's supremacy.

The tetrarchs were also united by family ties. Galerius divorced his wife and married Diocletian's daughter, Valeria. Similarly, Constantius separated from Helen, who had already given him a son, Constantine, and took to wife Maximian's stepdaughter, Theodora. In addition, each of the Caesars was adopted by his Augustus so that, in the future, as their sons, they could inherit their posts. And thus, each of the Caesars was simultaneously the son and the son-in-law of the Augustus to whom he was subordinated.

This division of power did not come from Diocletian's fearful pusillanimity, as Lactantius claims. On the contrary, by introducing the system, Diocletian acted like a true statesman concerned not so much with the glory and splendor of his own person but with the good of the state as a whole. Where the previous emperors had tried to hold everything in hand—as a result of which they lost everything easily and quickly—Diocletian demonstrated great political wisdom by sharing power. He showed that he was not petty and that he was prepared to take risks. He realized that the Empire was too large for one man to handle all of its responsibilities. The demands of the administrative and military challenges went far beyond the capabilities of even the most energetic individual.

For decades, the empire had been shaken by rebellions of provincial governors—people who were usually ambitious, talented, enterprising, and commanded both vast resources and large armies. They reached for power because they did not consider themselves inferior to those who had been put forward as emperors by the armies of other provinces. It was, therefore, necessary to shortcircuit this latent potential of rebellion by sharing power with a few of such men. The system of co-government was born out of necessity. It was an act of recognition and elevation to the rank of principle of a practice that had appeared sporadically in the past.

Another reform closely related to the introduction of the tetrarchy was a new administrative division of the state. Lactantius is right in saying that Diocletian broke up the provinces—but only partially right. That process had already begun much earlier, and Diocletian only took it to its logical conclusion. Before his reign, there had been fifty provinces; by the fourth century, their number increased to over a hundred.

What were the reasons for this new order? Lactantius, of course, has a ready answer: "to make state terror ubiquitous." But really, it was all about curbing the power of the governors and a fair distribution of burdens among individual lands of the empire. Several provinces formed a larger unit, the so-called diocese, *dioecesis*. There were six of them in the East and six in the West. The names of the western ones indicate what lands they covered: *Dioecesis Britanniarum*—Britain; *Galliarum*—northern and eastern France with the adjacent lands as far as the Rhine; *Vienensis*—Southern France and the basin of the Garonne; *Hispaniarum*—the whole Iberian Peninsula and Mauritania (northern Morocco today) in Africa; *Italiciana*—the whole of Italy and parts of the Alpine regions right up to the Danube; *Africae*—Algeria and Tunisia along with the Tripolitan part of Libya. It is striking that this division largely corresponds to the later distribution of nationalities in medieval Europe.

However, in the East, the situation was more complicated. *Dioecesis Pannoniarum* included parts of present-day Hungary, Serbia, and Austria; *Moesiarum*—the southern and eastern parts of Serbia, Albania, and Greece; *Thraciae*—Bulgaria, a part of Romania and today's European Turkey. Asia Minor was divided into two dioceses. The first, *Pontica*, covered its northern and eastern regions, while the second, *Asiana*, covered its West and South. The most extensive was the diocese of *Oriens* because within its borders lay Egypt, Libya, Palestine, Syria, and more—Cyprus, parts of Mesopotamia, and in Asia Minor—Cilicia and Isauria.

A diocese was headed by a *vicarius*, i.e., a vicar or "deputy." The name came from the fact that they represented the Praetorian Prefect. There were currently four of the latter, one at the side of each emperor.

Administrative and judicial power was separated from military power in most provinces, though this reform was only carried out fully by Constantine the Great.

Army and Taxes

Lactantius's statement that under Diocletian, the number of troops ballooned is also inaccurate. Yes, the number of tactical units and the total number of soldiers increased significantly, but probably by no more than half: where there had once been forty legions, now there were sixty. Still, the expansion had been necessary: it had proved impossible to safeguard the borders without it, and, indeed, it soon brought the desired results. The borders of the Empire were now secured along their entire length, from northern Britain, along the shores of the Rhine and the Danube to the Euphrates in the Middle East, to the cataracts of the Nile and the deserts of Africa. The civilian population breathed a sigh of relief: hordes of marauders pushed through the defense lines less often and never managed to venture too deep.

Diocletian also began reforming the structure of the army. This work was later continued by his successors, especially Constantine, and it is impossible to determine today exactly what specific measures each ruler introduced in this field. It seems, however, that it was Diocletian who first began to divide the troops into two categories. *Limitanei*, otherwise known as *ripenses*, were stationed on the borders of the empire and garrisoned its border fortifications, the so-called *limes*. Deeper within the empire were stationed powerful and highly mobile armies called *comitatenses* (because they belonged to the ruler's entourage, i.e., to his *comitatus*). The idea of introducing these two formations came from an astute assessment of the military situation: the Empire's borders were too long to man with strong units along their entire length. The *limitanei* were there only to hold off the first attack until a powerful field army, the *comitatus*, arrived to clean up. But let's bear in mind that this division only began to take its shape under Diocletian.

Lactantius's statement that each of the tetrarchs wanted to have an army larger than the armies of previous emperors is not really true. However, it is easy to point to the source of this claim: each of the four rulers now formed his own *comitatenses*. Lactantius, though his pamphlet oozes with hatred, does not fantasize: he distorts events and usually chooses the interpretation least favorable to Diocletian, but a careful analysis shows that his information usually reflects reality to some extent.

The third factor that helped bring the military situation under control was the expansion of border fortifications. Many previous emperors had contributed to the fortification, but Diocletian's works in this area are impressive. We will return to this topic in due course.

These vast expenditures on the army and the border fortifications, on the one hand, and on the expanded bureaucratic apparatus, on the other, had to be matched by an increase of revenues. However, taxes were not so much increased as systematized and more strictly enforced to provide the state with regular revenue and spread its burden more evenly across the population. The system took into account different factors, and data about it are sparse, but the general rules went as follows:

Every landowner paid tax, usually in kind, that is, in agricultural produce (*annona*). The amount depended i) on the quantity and quality of land he held which was expressed in certain tax units (*jugatio*); ii) on the number of laborers (*capitatio*); and iii) the type of crops and/or farm animals it raised. Every fifteen years, the amount due was revised on the basis of a universal census. The first census was conducted in 297. Starting with the reign of Diocletian, taxes were also collected in Italy, which, as the cradle of the Empire, had, until then, been free from any duties. Henceforth, northern Italy paid normal land tax (*annona*), whereas the south of the peninsula was assessed with contributions for the needs of the city of Rome.

Contrary to the reports of Lactantius, it seems that the general population welcomed the new system as a relief. We should remember that similar tributes had been imposed on the inhabitants of most provinces for centuries but without clear rules concerning amounts due or frequency or payment dates. The new criteria were harsh, and there certainly were cases of enforcement that were too strict due to officials' arbitrariness or local crop failures. The treasury was implacable and demanded taxes in full, regardless of the conditions. It was also sometimes the case, as Lactantius says that in some areas, tenants abandoned their land, but similar phenomena had occurred in the past, more often and on a larger scale. So, his information is only partially true.

Behind the decision to collect all taxes in kind lay the inflationary monetary policy that had been practiced by the Imperial government for generations: a wholesale debasement of currency consisting in a dramatic reduction of the silver content of the coin. (The Roman equivalent of the modern phenomenon of "printing of money"). In the absence of modern central banking with its interest rate and bank reserve tools capable of adjusting the money supply in the economy, the Roman monetary crisis could only be remedied by replacing bad money with good money wholesale. Understanding this, Diocletian increased the number of mints, almost doubling their number, and he minted large amounts of good gold, silver, and copper coin. The basic unit of accounting was the *denarius*. Despite endless debates, numismatists have not been able to determine the size of coin this unit should be identified with.

The emperor did not stop at this. Like some rulers before him and very many after him, he attempted to manage the economy with top-down orders. His office now prepared a long and detailed schedule of maximum allowable prices of goods and services. We remember that Lactantius reserved his sharpest words of critique for this measure, which he considered cruel and impractical, but we should ask ourselves what Diocletian's goals were when he imposed his price schedule. We happen to have the Emperor's answer in his own words. It survived in various inscriptions, along with extensive fragments of the price schedule itself and with a long introduction.

Diocletian:
The Schedule of Maximum Prices

It would take a stone heart and a perverse sense of morality to deny that both wholesale and retail prices have reached levels of unprecedented greed and extortion in recent years, levels unjustified by the supply of goods or the yield of harvests. For this reason, we decided to take the following action: not to mandate fixed prices for goods—because such a decision would be unfair to those provinces which enjoy low prices—but rather to mandate maximum prices so that when a wave of high prices should emerge, greed, which otherwise knows no moderation, may find its limit in the guidelines of the law. Therefore, it is our will that the maximum prices given in the attached list be known and respected across the country. This does not deny the blessing of cheapness to those places which enjoy an abundance of things.

At the same time, we declare that anyone who acts contrary to this edict shall be punished by death. Let no one consider such punishment too severe, for it is easy to avoid by simply observing the limits set herein. Nor shall those be spared who, finding themselves in possession of articles necessary for life, hide them after this edict has been published. In truth, in such cases, the punishment should be even more severe because causing an artificial shortage of goods is an even more serious crime than violating the maximum prices themselves.

Therefore, we appeal to the conscience of all to observe this decree with the necessary obedience and diligence, as it serves the common good. All the more so because it seeks to aid not individual cities, peoples, and provinces but the entire world, for whose detriment an extremely small group driven by greed is working with incessant industry: a group that will not be satisfied by the abundance of everything in our times, or even by the attainment of the riches that constitute the goal of their efforts.[7]

After this fatherly admonition comes a long list of goods and services, and their maximum prices are given in *denarii*. We will see parts of this list in one of the following chapters. For the moment, let us only note one thing: the emperor's intentions were praiseworthy. All the same, Lactantius is right: the results of the decree proved disastrous. The strict penalties did work, and no one observed the maximum prices. Instead, trade went underground. Speculation flourished, and corruption of the official apparatus became widespread. Meanwhile, the shortage of goods on the market became even more severe. The law, although never officially repealed, died a natural death of non-

---

[7] *De pretiis rerum venalium*, ed. Th. Mommsen, Berlin 1893.

enforcement. It remains one of the prime exhibits in the—unfortunately, ever richer—museum of praiseworthy regulations promulgated against the grain of human nature and the laws of the market.[8]

Notable Buildings

Perhaps the most tendentious is Lactantius's criticism of Diocletian's construction projects. Yes, the emperor built a lot and fast, which was typical of all his actions. But—this is clear even from the cursory list given by Lactantius—most of the buildings served public good—either the civilian administration or the general population. The emperor built basilicas—huge public halls in which public meetings, court hearings, and even markets were held; established new mints to address the shortage of good coinage; and armorer's workshops to supply the expanding army. Lactantius also completely ignores another class of public works of Diocletian, which were initiated out of concern for the security of the Empire: border fortifications.

Many previous emperors had built them at considerable expense. Diocletian, however, vastly expanded the fortifications not only along the border but also in depth. Apart from expanding the lines of ramparts and walls, he also built a whole network of forts, camps, and fortresses within the interior and connected them with newly built roads. Yes, he often used preexisting structures and plans as the basis of his projects; however, no one has ever done this work on such a massive scale. The remains on the Syrian-Arab border are particularly impressive; they run the whole length of the desert from the Euphrates to the borders of Egypt. Their scale careful design can only be assessed today with the help of satellite photos.

Of course, Diocletian also built imperial residences, and here

---

[8] Those words were published in 1970, in an environment of a general shortage of consumer goods and raging inflation in Poland which led to the December 1970 strikes and the fall of the Gomułka regime.

he graciously singled out certain cities. We have already mentioned his palace near Solin, in today's Croatia; its ruins now grace the picturesque town of Split and are visited by crowds of tourists from all over the world. The emperor also undertook great works in Nicomedia, a city in Asia Minor on the coast of the Propontis, or the Sea of Marmara. This was perhaps partly due to the fact that he had been elevated to the throne by the army near Nicomedia and partly justified by the city's excellent location on the borders of Asia and Europe and on the sea route to the Black Sea.

Even though he never stayed there very long, Diocletian built many great public buildings in Nicomedia. And while his court moved constantly from the Danube to the Euphrates to the Nile to oversee the affairs of the vast Empire, many official acts and ceremonies were performed in Nicomedia. And thus, it could be said that Diocletian initiated the process of transferring the center of the empire to the East. Bear in mind, that almost opposite Nicomedia, on the European side of Propontis, lay the city of Byzantium—that Byzantium which would soon change its name and take center stage in history.

Meanwhile, Rome remained the formal capital of the empire, and both Diocletian and Maximian made great efforts to enhance it. The Roman Forum, destroyed by the great fire of 283, was restored. So were the famous Julian Basilica and the Curia—the meeting hall of the Senate—as well as Pompey's theater. The great waterworks called Aqua Marcia were expanded. A monumental fountain was built on the Aventine Hill, fed by the waters of three aqueducts. But Diocletian's most famous work in Rome remains the huge thermal baths bearing his name. It was a colossal complex of marble rooms where users could swim in pools with hot and cold water and practice sports. The baths' impressive remains stand to this day near the main railway station; the station takes its name from it—Stazione Termini, *Termini* meaning "Thermal Baths." Since the Renaissance, one of its vast rooms has housed the magnificent church of Santa Maria degli Angeli; in others, the parts of the collections of the Roman National Museum are now exhibited.

Writing about Diocletian's buildings in Nicomedia,

Lactantius makes a sarcastic remark: "He wanted his Nicomedia to be equal to Rome." Yet Lactantius himself moved to that city—and did so thanks to Diocletian. How did that happen?

On the Social Position of the Roman Intelligentsia

Lactantius came from North Africa, from what is now Algeria or Tunisia. The cities of Africa had been completely Romanized and had long given many great writers to Roman literature; it is enough to name just two: Apuleius and Tertullian.

When he moved to Asia Minor, Lactantius was about fifty. He had been summoned to Nicomedia, the emperor's main residence, because he had established his reputation as a great Latin stylist. The state administration still used Latin as its sole language and needed teachers who could educate a Latin-speaking bureaucratic cadre in a Greek-speaking city.

Lactantius appears to be a zealous Christian in his writings, but his theology is shallow, and his faith does not blaze with fanatical zeal. Yet, he does attack and mock the opponents of his religion, which raises an interesting question: did Lactantius arrive in Nicomedia as a Christian, or did he become one in the East? It is difficult to answer this because all his surviving works date from the later years of his life, i.e., from the period in Nicomedia and later in Trier. Yet we would like to know whether the emperor's advisers, who summoned a lecturer of rhetoric from distant African provinces, were aware of his religious beliefs. If Lactantius had come from Africa as a Christian, he might have been one of the students of Arnobius.[9]

---

[9] Arnobius was an early Christian apologist of Berber origin. According to Jerome's Chronicle, Arnobius, before his conversion, was a distinguished Numidian rhetorician at Sicca Veneria, a major Christian center in Proconsular Africa, and owed his conversion to a premonitory dream. His *Adversus nationes* (*Against the Pagans*) was composed in response to arguments justifying Diocletian's persecution

Be that as it may, one thing is certain: Lactantius was not only a worshipper of Christ but also a worshipper of the beauty of the Latin language, the treasures of its literature, and the heritage of its past. In this regard, the imperial administration chose the right man.

In fact, Lactantius could be considered a fairly typical representative of the *intelligentsia* of his times, i.e., the social class that lives by selling the services of its mind and has no other productive assets or skills. Some sociologists talk today, and rightly so, of the *intelligentsia* in the Middle Ages; we are all the more justified to speak of a large social stratum in the era of the Empire—composed of representatives of various professions—which can also be defined in this manner.

First of all, this *intelligentsia* included teachers. Whole armies of teachers existed in third-century Rome, teachers of various subjects at lower and higher schools. The most numerous were those who taught the elements of reading, writing, arithmetic, and geometry. Then came the so-called grammarians, who taught intermediate grades; they taught mainly literature. The third and highest level of education was the study of rhetoric, which was closely connected with the practice of law. Schools, especially at lower levels, were basically private. However, individual cities had long maintained salaried "grammarians," and emperors funded "chairs" for professors of rhetoric and philosophy in some centers. In addition, legislation often exempted teachers from taxes due to municipalities and the state.

This universality of teaching is astonishing and commands respect. The need for it was understood by all social circles. Even the poor did not spare money to ensure the education of their children.

A period of bloody wars, barbarian invasions, and economic collapse in the third century did not diminish the significance of education. On the contrary, the rising bureaucratization of the state, which had already begun to manifest itself at that time and matured

---

of Christians by claiming that Christians had brought the wrath of the gods on Ancient Rome. Revilo P. Oliver describes him as "a practitioner of the turgid and coarse style that is called African."

under Diocletian, meant that demand for human resources for the administrative apparatus continued to grow.

How much did teachers earn? We have various clues in this matter, but the most valuable information comes from—Diocletian's schedule of maximum prices. We know that the prices for what we would call "scarce goods" or "luxury goods" were not generally respected, yet when it came to teachers' pay, the table has to reflect in some way the structure of wages and living costs of the time. The schedule determined the remuneration of teachers of various subjects and grades per student per month; the monetary unit was the denarius.

And so:

A teacher of reading and writing:	50d
of gymnastics:	50d
of arithmetic:	75d
of stenography:	75d
of architecture:	100d
of literature:	200d
of geometry:	200d
of rhetoric:	250d

For comparison, here are the wages of manual workers:

An agricultural worker	25d per day plus meals
A bricklayer	50d per day plus meals
A carpenter	50d per day plus meals
A donkey driver	25d per day plus meals
A wall painter	75d per day plus meals
An artistic painter	150d per day plus meals
A hairdresser	per haircut 2d

And here are the costs of foodstuffs:

A pound of pork	12d
A pound of beef	8d
A pair of good quality men's shoes	120d
A pair of good quality women's shoes	60d

Ten cucumbers	4d
Ten first-grade apples	4d
One egg	1d

Wine was expensive: the best sorts cost 30d for one *sextarius* (a little over half a liter), and the poorest sorts cost 2d.

This would seem to mean that teachers, even those of the highest categories, were poorly remunerated. If he had only ten students, a rhetorician would earn only three times as much per month as a donkey driver, who was provided with daily subsistence to boot. This seems to undermine the claim to the high respect in which learning was held at the time. But the contradiction is only apparent because history knows many eras when teaching was common and respected, and yet teachers' salaries were scandalously low.

However, the *intelligentsia* consisted not only of teachers. Its largest cohort was government officials. We have already mentioned the expansion of the bureaucracy, and we will return to this topic in the future. Lawyers, both judges and attorneys, had a close relationship with the official apparatus. The latter's fees were, according to Diocletian's tariff, quite good: 250 *denarii* for bringing a case; 1,000 for conducting it. Lawyers earned a lot thanks to the confusing thicket of contradictory laws, decrees, rescripts, and court decisions. This arose as a result of centuries of work by lawyers, and the imperial chancellery was particularly fruitful. Becoming familiar with the jungle of regulations required high qualifications. Therefore, lawyers were consulted even in non-contentious matters.

The *intelligentsia* also included architects and doctors, artists, actors, and even priests of various religions and deities; some of the latter were, for their times, highly educated people.

Returning to Lactantius: as the above shows, his income depended on the number of students he had. But the inhabitants of Greek Nicomedia did not show much interest in Latin literature or rhetoric. One source clearly states that Lactantius had very few students and, therefore, devoted himself to writing.

The disappointment that Nicomedia must have caused

Lactantius could perhaps partly explain his hatred towards Diocletian. But he writes similarly, and perhaps even more critically, about two of his co-rulers.

Maximian

Here is Lactantius's opinion concerning the second Augustus, the ruler of the West:

> What can we say about Diocletian's brother, Maximian, nicknamed Herculean? The two were like peas in the pod. After all, they could never have become bound by such faithful friendship if it had not been for their similarity of thought and desire and the general compatibility of their views. They differed from each other only in that Diocletian was more greedy but also more timid, while Maximian was less greedy but more enterprising—not, of course, in doing good, but in all kinds of evil. He ruled the capital of the Empire and Italy, as well as its richest provinces: Africa and Spain. Therefore, he did not have to watch over the treasury as diligently as Diocletian, for he had plenty of wealth.
>
> And should he ever be short of cash, he had to hand the richest senators, who were easy to accuse with the help of planted informers of plotting anti-government conspiracies. In this way, to put it figuratively, the brightest stars of the Senate were constantly executed and dispossessed, while Maximian's treasury was kept full of blood-stained specie. This monster's lust was directed not only toward men, which is in itself disgusting and deserving condemnation but also drove him to rape the daughters of the most eminent families. Wherever he went during his travels, girls were immediately torn from their parents' arms and delivered to him to serve him. He believed that his personal happiness and the good fortune of the government depended on not denying his lust and criminal debauchery.[10]

---

[10] Lactantius, 8

So much for Lactantius. For all we know, this could be a true portrait, but we should remember that Roman rulers were often accused of sexual depravity; it became a permanent feature of a tyrant's portrait because it elicited outrage and condemnation, and yet its credibility was impossible to check. It is also worth noting an interesting gradation in the accusations that Lactantius brings against the emperor: the alleged fact that he took into his bed girls from aristocratic families outraged him more than his homosexual interests. This judgment reveals, in an almost humorous way, the cult in which the humble teacher of rhetoric had the higher social classes, especially the distinguished families of the Roman Senate.

Maximian, like Diocletian, came from a very poor family. He was born near Sirmium, on the lower Sava River, in what is now Serbia. He later built a beautiful palace in the town where he was born. Yet, scores of years later, a tradition survived that his parents had worked there as manual laborers. Maximian owed his career to his early contact with Diocletian. In 286, he suppressed a dangerous peasant uprising in Gaul; in the same year, probably on March 1, he received from Diocletian the dignity of Caesar and, several months later, Augustus. As we already know, he resided in Italy, mainly in Aquileia and Milan, for Rome was increasingly becoming only the symbolic capital of the Empire. However, Maximian often traveled to Gaul and Spain and even to Africa, where he achieved great victories and reorganized the defense of the local provinces against attacks by desert nomads.

Galerius

The Caesar at Diocletian's side was Galerius, the ruler of the Balkan provinces. His full name was Gaius Galerius Maximianus. We have already heard that he divorced his first wife to marry Valeria, Diocletian's daughter, thus cementing his political position. Lactantius's feelings for him are best shown in his own words:

But Galerius was the worst of all, not only worse than the two tyrants [that is, Diocletian and Maximian] but, in general, worse than anyone who has ever existed. There was some natural barbarism and savagery in this beast, features completely foreign to Roman blood. And no wonder: his mother came from the Transdanubian region [Dacia, that is, today's Romania]. When the Carpi invaded the area, she crossed the river and fled to the province of Dacia Nova.

The figure of Galerius reflected his character. The emperor was tall and massive, swollen and bloated to terrifying proportions. His words and actions, as well as his appearance, aroused fear and terror in everyone. Even his father-in-law, Diocletian, was afraid of him. The reason for this fear was this: Narseh, king of the Persians,[11] had intended to occupy our eastern provinces; for this purpose, he gathered a huge army. He was encouraged to go on this expedition by the memorable example of the victories of his grandfather, King Shapur.

Whenever he was faced with a difficult situation, Diocletian became fearful and depressed. In this case, he became very afraid that he would meet the fate of Emperor Valerian [whom King Shapur had defeated and taken into captivity]. That's why he did not dare to set out against the Persians himself. Therefore, he sent Galerius to Armenia and remained in the back himself, watching how the situation might develop. Meanwhile, Galerius lured the barbarians into an ambush. They normally go to war with everything they have, so the sheer size of their army immobilizes them and burdens them with a tremendous baggage train. Thus, Galerius won an easy victory. He forced King Narseh to flee and returned with enormous spoils.

All this made him proud and conceited. The title of Caesar was no longer enough for him. When he heard that it had been used in one of Diocletian's letters addressed to him, he shouted with a fierce expression on his face and in a terrible voice:

"How long am I to remain just a Caesar?"

---

[11] The seventh Sasanian King of Kings of Iran, 293-303.

From then on, he acted with incredible arrogance. He wanted it to be believed and proclaimed that he was the son of Mars, a second Romulus. He thereby allowed it that his mother, whose name was Romula, was an adulteress—so long that he could be considered a descendant of the gods.[12]

These words require some explanation.

First of all, it should be noted that the assessments of Galerius given by other writers of this period are much more favorable. Unfortunately, those mentions are short and do not allow for a proper confrontation with the account of Lactantius.

Secondly, we must say a few words about the war with Persia. It was probably fought in AD 297 and did end in a Roman victory, mainly thanks to Galerius's capable command. It was a success so famous that Lactantius could not *not* mention it. However, he tried to belittle Galerius's merits, implying that the Ceasar won his victory thanks to an ambush and the general stodginess of the Persian army. And he omits to say that Galerius captured the treasury of King Narseh as well as his entire harem.

Lactantius's claim that during this campaign, Diocletian cowardly stayed at the rear is also not true. His army secured Galerius' right flank on the Syrian front and, at the same time, provided cover for the southern provinces in case the Persians should suddenly change the direction of their advance. And thus, even in a passage devoted to Galerius, Lactantius finds the opportunity to badmouth Diocletian.

It is significant that the rhetorician from Nicomedia does not say a single word about a fact well-known from many preserved sources: in the first phase of the war with Persia, Galerius suffered a smarting defeat when, contrary to Diocletian's recommendations, he attacked the enemy with an insufficiently large force.

When Galerius returned from Armenia after his great victory, Diocletian received him with great solemnity in Antioch, the capital city of Syria. Yet, it seems that a little earlier, there had been some conflict between the Augustus and his Caesar in connection with the

---

campaign. It seems that Diocletian, cautious and farsighted, reigned in the belligerent ambitions of Galerius, who wanted to go further East, deep into Iran. In any case, the Caesar did not obtain the title of Augustus at that time. However, the fame of the victory made an indelible impression on his contemporaries. It was said, both then and even decades later, that Galerius had attained feats comparable to the monumental conquests of Alexander the Great.

He himself zealously promoted these hyperboles. Moreover, he saw himself—and many others saw him—as the reincarnation of the king of the Macedonians from seven centuries ago. At the same time, his admirers also spread another legend: it was centered around the fact that Galerius's mother was named Romula, and the founder of Rome was named Romulus. And since myth had it that the father of Romulus was Mars, Galerius also claimed Mars as his father. The God had apparently approached Romula in the form of a snake or a dragon. In keeping with this line, the following inscription appeared on Galerius's coins: *Marti patri semper victori* (To Father Mars, always victorious).

Constantius

Of the four tetrarchs, only one found favor in the eyes of Lactantius. The author writes about him briefly but significantly: "I leave out Constantius because he was different from the others; only he was worthy to rule the world."[13]

Other ancient sources also give positive witness to Constantius. A very interesting characterization is given by Eutropius, a historian who lived in the mid-fourth century:

> He was an outstanding man, full of great civic virtues. He wanted the inhabitants of the provinces and private people in general to prosper and did not seek to increase the revenues of the state

---

[13] Lactantius, 12

46

treasury. He used to say: "It is better for public resources to be in individual possession than to be locked up in the treasury." He managed his court so modestly that when he hosted a feast for a larger group of friends on the occasion of some holiday, his tables were laid with silverware borrowed from his neighbors. The inhabitants of Gaul not only loved him but even worshiped him, mainly because, under his rule, they escaped both the police methods of Diocletian and the choleric recklessness of Maximian.[14]

Constantius was raised to the dignity of Caesar on March 1, AD 293. He owed his career to his military talents, but it is difficult to determine its course today. It seems that just before receiving Caesar's purple, he had held the office of the Praetorian Prefect.

His full name was Gaius Flavius Julius Constantius. When Maximian made him Caesar and adopted him, he added to his name the divine nickname of Herculius. It is probable that Constantius—despite his noble name—came from a poor family. Later, he tried to add splendor to his descent by suggesting a connection with Emperor Claudius II Gothicus, who had died in AD 270 and became famous for his victory over the Goths. It seems, however, that that genealogy was an invention of court flatterers. We will come back to this matter later.

What is known for certain is that Constantius was born in today's Serbia. We remember, of course, that the other three tetrarchs also came from the northern Balkans. At the time, those provinces provided the empire with its best soldiers and its most ardent patriots. The four rulers were, therefore, united by the community of the motherland in the stricter sense of the word as well.

While still a young officer, Constantius became involved with a woman named Helen, the owner of an inn (or just a servant at one) in the city of Naissos, in the province of Moesia Superior. This is present-day Niš in Serbia. The couple's only son, Constantine (*Constantinus*), was born there on February 27. Later, when he became emperor, this date was celebrated solemnly throughout the Empire

---

[14] Eurtropius X, 1

and was therefore recorded in calendars. However, it is difficult to determine the year of his birth. Our data is contradictory. We have to settle for an estimate: before AD 280, possibly around 272.

Constantius's marriage to Helen was informal, but the formality of marriage was not strictly observed at the time, especially among the military. In any case, the fact that Constantine was born "out of wedlock" (as future generations would say) never brought embarrassment or difficulty to Constantine: he was always considered the natural heir to all of his father's inheritance.

Constantius separated from Helen before he was raised to the rank of Caesar—perhaps when he started to hold higher offices. It is possible that he married Theodora, Maximian's stepdaughter already then, perhaps when Constantine was still a child. But Constantine remained very devoted to his mother all his life and demonstrated his devotion publicly.

The union of Constantius and Theodora was perhaps a happy one—if we are to judge from the number of offspring. The new wife gave to her husband as many as six children: three sons—Dalmatius, Julius Constantius, and Hannibalianus, and three daughters: Constantia, Anastasia, and Eutropia. The name of the second daughter is significant. At the time, it was used only by Jews and Christians because it supposedly betrayed one's religious affiliation: it was derived from the Greek word *anastasis*, meaning "resurrection." On this basis, we could propose that Empress Theodora had some sympathies for one or the other religion. But which one? Perhaps she favored Jews since it is known that her mother—Theodora Eutropia— after whom the couple's third daughter was named—had generously supported Jews.[15]

Constantius himself was a zealous worshiper of a deity called *Sol Invictus*, i.e., the Invincible Sun. This cult had long been widespread in the ranks of the Roman army and in certain circles of

---

[15] Aurelius Victor, *Epitome de Caesaribus* (39.25) tells us that Theodora Eutropia came from Syria and that her first husband, Afranius Hannibalianus, was Syrian. (Translator's note).

the educated classes.[16] Young Constantine, as we will see, was also among the followers of *Sol Invictus* and, for many years, promoted the cult among his subjects.

It is not known where Constantine spent his boyhood years: with his father or away from him. In any case, we can assume that he spent them in the Balkan provinces—which is suggested by the obvious attachment to those parts he was to demonstrate in later years. However, soon after 293, Constantine was sent to the court of Diocletian; his mother probably accompanied him. The first Augustus undoubtedly sent out an elaborate invitation: the young man was to be educated at the emperor's side, learning about the business of the Empire. In truth, Constantine became a hostage: he served as a guarantee of his father's loyalty.

Shortly after receiving the title of Caesar, Constantius performed heroic deeds. He recovered Britain and the coast of Gaul, where the self-proclaimed emperor Carausius had ruled for several years. He defeated the Franks on the lower Rhine. He made great strides in the economic reconstruction of Gaul, which had been devastated by barbarian invasions and tenant farmer uprisings. He settled craftsmen imported from Britain in the cities of Gaul and thousands of Germanic prisoners in the villages. In later years, after a short stay in Italy, he again went to war against the Franks and defeated the Alemanni.

Meanwhile, his son traveled with Diocletian through the eastern provinces of the Empire.

On The Danube, Nile, and Euphrates

Throughout AD 293 and until November AD 294, Diocletian's court resided in the northern Balkans. As did Galerius. Both tetrarchs were

---

[16] Emperor Aurelian revived this cult in AD 274 and promoted Sol Invictus as the chief god of the empire. From that point on, Sol was of supreme importance, and often appeared on imperial coinage.

constantly moving from one town to another throughout the lands of today's Serbia, Croatia, Hungary, Bulgaria, and European Turkey. The main reason for this tireless mobility was their military campaigns. Diocletian personally inspected the border areas, which were constantly under threat of invasion from across the Danube: it was necessary to expand the system of fortifications and military roads. To frighten off the hostile barbarians, he and Galerius conducted a series of short, sudden raids across the great river against the tribes of Sarmatians, Carpi, Goths, and Gepids.

Later, in spring 297, long after Diocletian's departure, Galerius defeated the Peuci and the Carpi, who had crossed the frozen Danube and penetrated deep into the Roman provinces. It is noteworthy, however, that no attempt was ever made to recover the former Roman possessions north of the lower Danube—the province of Dacia, that is, today's Romania, which had been lost almost thirty years earlier. All action was limited to repelling raids on the Danubian *limes* and, at most, a few short-term cross-river raids.

Another reason for the constant movement of the imperial court was difficulty with supply. The ruler was accompanied by thousands of people: servants, officials, military units. Procuring, storing, and transporting large amounts of food was not an easy task, especially in territories devastated by wars. The local population was required to supply not only food but also housing and means of transport—this system had long been regulated by laws and decrees of many previous emperors. Thus, the court took care to distribute its burden evenly among different districts by constantly moving from place to place.

During these journeys in 293 and 294, Diocletian stopped twice in Byzantium on the Bosphorus. It was probably then that young Constantine saw the city for the first time—a city which was in time to receive his name and bear it for a thousand years.

Diocletian spent the winter 294-295 in Nicomedia. Then, he moved south through Asia Minor to Syria. By 295, he was already in Egypt. He had to devote a lot of time and energy to the affairs of that province as it was thrashing in the convulsions of a large-scale rebellion. Riots began in Upper Egypt and later spread to Lower Egypt and eventually to Alexandria.

The reasons for the uprising were primarily economic, as the Roman authorities placed particularly heavy burdens on this fertile land. Alexandria had to be besieged for eighteen months. It was recovered only at the beginning of 297, and only because its fresh water supply was cut off. The emperor punished the leaders of the uprising ruthlessly and then introduced administrative and military reforms in Egypt.

As we remember, in 297 came the great threat from the East, in the person of the Persian king Narseh. We remember how Galerius, sent against him, won a great victory after some initial setbacks. Meanwhile, Diocletian stood on the middle Euphrates in case of a sudden Persian attack in that direction. Ultimately, the war brought territorial gains in northern Mesopotamia and the recognition of the Roman protectorate over Armenia. Following the peace settlement, the eastern border enjoyed fifty years of peace.

Diocletian's activities during those few years certainly greatly influenced the mind of the honorary hostage at his side, the young Prince Constantine. The mere sight of so many lands, so diverse, colorful, and rich, must have been a great experience for a teenage boy. We remember that he was born in Naissos. And while that city, located on a tributary of the Morava River, was the military and administrative center of the province of Upper Moesia, it could not compare with the metropolises of the neighboring Balkan provinces, not to mention the magnificent capitals of Asia Minor, Syria, and Egypt. Centuries and millennia had decorated those cities with monumental buildings and works of art, and they brimmed with the riches of economic and cultural life. In this respect, the East was greatly superior to the West, even to Italy and Gaul. Before arriving at Diocletian's court, Constantine may have visited some of the western provinces with his father, but he was still a child then.

And yet, amazingly enough, the Balkans remained Constantine's true and beloved homeland. We know too little about the emperor's personal life to explain it. It has been suggested that

Constantine was attached to those places because they were the setting for the earliest memories of his youth. Whatever the reason, the fact remains that although the duties of rulership would keep him in other countries for long periods of time, after his final victory, he established his residence in a city located on the border of the Balkans and Asia Minor.

But perhaps even more important than all the lands of the East passing before his eyes was the direct contact with the court of Diocletian and, therefore, with the life and functioning of the heart of the Empire.

Offices and Ceremonies

According to a popular view, Diocletian was the first Roman emperor to introduce a new style of court ceremonial, one closely modeled on the Persian. The ruler appeared in a purple robe, dripping with gold and precious stones. Only the highest dignitaries were allowed to appear before him, and special officials kept order and silence in the hall. Ushers parted the heavy curtain that hid him from sight. Everyone, even the closest family members, fell on their knees and humbly kissed the hem of the emperor's robe. This act of homage was called "adoration" (*adoratio*) and had an almost religious character. Even granting an audience, let alone allowing someone to touch the emperor's garment with their lips, was considered an act of imperial grace.

During deliberations, even with the officials of the highest rank, only the emperor sat; everyone else stood respectfully. This was how the Imperial Council came to be known as *consistorium*, from the Latin expression *consistere*, meaning "standing together." There are even such images on coins: Diocletian and Maximian sitting on thrones and the gods Jupiter and Hercules standing next to them, placing wreaths on the heads of the rulers.

To understand the full meaning of such scenes—mortals

sitting before standing gods, we must remember that early emperors stood respectfully before the Senate and even before individual senators. But the current rulers considered themselves more honorable than the gods.

Moreover, great care was taken to ensure that a halo of sanctity surrounded all things imperial. Hence, there was an increasingly frequent use of the term *sacer*—"sacred"—when speaking about anything having to do with the emperor. It became customary to say: sacred decrees, sacred signature, sacred letter, sacred palace, sacred quarters, and even—sacred munificence (the treasury).

During the first three centuries of the empire, everyone—including the emperors—had done their best to preserve the appearance that the emperor was only the most senior official of the Republic, merely the chairman of the Senate and the Popular Assembly. For this reason, historians have traditionally called that system "the Principate," from the Latin word *princeps*, meaning "leader," but referring to the system instituted by Diocletian—and everything that followed—they have used the term "the Dominate," a word derived from the Latin *dominus*, meaning master, and indicating that the emperor became a full-faced autocrat, dispensing henceforth with all polite Republican pretense.

These views, however, require some modification.[17] The reign of Diocletian was no doubt crucial for the development of new political concepts, but it was not a sudden transformation. Rather, it was the culmination of a process that had gradually built up over the centuries. Even the court ceremonial—perhaps not so important in itself, but nevertheless a symbol of deeper phenomena—had developed under previous emperors. This is evidenced by both written testimony and iconographic material, that is, scenes and images on sculptures, base reliefs, paintings, and especially coins. Costume, adoration, the nimbus of divinity—all these elements of the cult of the

---

[17] See A. Alfoldi, *Die Ausgestaltung des monarchischen Zeremoniells am romischen Kaiserhofe,* Mitteilungen des deutschen archeologischen Instituts, Romische Abteilung, XLIX 1934, p. 1-118

person of the ruler were present, although in varying degrees, already during the second century and occasionally even earlier.

It is to Diocletian's credit that he systematized all these *ad hoc* forms—just as he tried to create logical and orderly structures in all areas of the administration.

And how did young Constantine view the new ceremonial at court? We have no clues on this matter—no statement of Constantine himself. Yet, it seems that the splendor of the imperial court made an indelible impression on him because, when he later became the sole ruler, he not only retained all the ceremonial he had seen at the court of Diocletian but embellished it further and thereby helped solidify a rigid court etiquette that for centuries dominated the Late Roman Empire and later Byzantium.

But the emperor was surrounded by more than just courtiers. The ceremonial was only a majestic facade meant to inspire naïve fear and adoration among those looking in from the outside. The actual brain and engine room of the empire were the numerous secretariats and ministries, civilian and military, the so-called *officia*. Their managers worked out of the imperial palace.

All important decisions were made during the meetings of these high officials. We will discuss the very complicated structure of the offices later on in this book, but the effects of their work have already been presented.

It was indeed a tireless activity. It seemed to many that Diocletian was consumed by an obsession with total change; that he wanted to tear down everything in order to build a wholy new edifice of the Empire from scratch. But that wasn't the case. Diocletian was a conservative by temperament, a man sincerely attached to Rome's great past. Yes, he carried out reforms, but only those that, in his understanding, were necessary to *preserve* the legacy of the past.

We have a telling example of this in the form of his *Edict on the Manichaeans*. It is well worth paying attention to, as it will help us understand the emperor's religious policy.

Manichaeans

In the spring of AD 297—on March 31, to be exact, that is, mere days after the recapture of Alexandria, Diocletian's chancellery issued an edict, the essential content of which—after removing the rhetorical embellishments and repetitions—reads as follows:

> The peace we brought to the empire has encouraged some people to overstep the measure set by nature. They introduce a confusion of completely meaningless and repulsive beliefs, and since they are allowed to act with impunity, they attract a multitude of followers. But the immortal gods had already, in their kindness, deigned to reveal to many illustrious and wise men of the past what is good and true; and this should not be opposed or resisted or reformed. New beliefs should not overthrow the old ones, for it is the greatest crime to reject what our ancestors have established. Therefore, we make every effort to punish the hard-hearted perversity of wicked people who oppose some newfangled new faiths to the old beliefs and, on the basis of some arbitrary novel fancy, spurn the mercy of the old gods.
>
> Manichaeans came to us from Persia, a hostile country. They arrived in recent times bringing odd new notions. They commit many crimes.
>
> They create confusion among our peaceful people, causing great upheaval in the cities. It is to be feared that, in time, they will pervert our innocent people, our humble and peaceful citizenry, and our whole social system with the venom of their accursed customs and repulsive Persian laws.
>
> We, therefore, order that the Manichaean leaders and their abominable writings be consumed by fire. Their followers, should they continue to behave in their current acrimonious ways, shall pay for it with their heads also, and their estates will be confiscated by the state treasury. If any officials or eminent citizens join the feckless, hateful, and unspeakable sect or further the teachings of the Persians, they, too, will lose their property to the treasury, while they themselves will be sentenced to hard labor in the mines. This blight

of wickedness must be extirpated from this happiest of all ages![18]

Who were the Manichaeans? Why did the emperor attack them so violently? What were their crimes?

Mani had been born around AD 215 in southern Babylonia. He came from an old, aristocratic Iranian family. His father took a keen interest in the matters of religion and may have associated himself with one of the communities of the Gnostics. There were many such communities throughout the Middle East at the time. The Greek word *gnosis*, or "knowledge," is used to describe a very complex and diverse religious current, which arose in the first century AD and quickly gained many followers but never formed a compact denominational system or established an ecclesiastical organization. The teachings of the Gnostics were varied and contradictory, consistent only in the core belief: that the path to salvation led through mystical knowledge of the hidden, ultimate, divine Truth. There were disagreements as to what the truth was or how it could be known.

Around the year 240, Mani traveled to India, where he came into contact with Buddhism. He then returned to his homeland. He faithfully served the great Persian king of the Sassanid dynasty, Shapur. It seems he even held a high court dignity during that king's expedition against the Roman Emperor Valerian. The expedition ended, as we recall, with the brilliant Persian victory in 260 and the capture of the Emperor himself.

While serving his king, Mani developed a lively missionary activity and, in time, became the founder of a new religion that combined elements of old Iranian beliefs with Gnostic mysticism and some Christian views. According to him, the universe was a stage for the primordial and continuous struggle between the forces of Light and Darkness. The struggle played out in every human being, for the human mind contained particles of light imprisoned in matter by Satan. It was man's duty to liberate these elements of light and

---

[18]*Collectio librorum iuris anteiustiniani,* ed.. Kruger-Mommsen, Leipzig 1890, p. 187

goodness. To this end, it was necessary to lead a godly life and pursue various ascetic practices. Periodically, great teachers arose in the world—Zoroaster, Moses, Buddha, Mani—to remind us of that challenge.

Initially, the Persian kings were quite tolerant of Mani's activities. Later, however, the prophet was imprisoned and may have been crucified. But by then, his teachings had already found many followers, and now they were carried forth to all parts of the world. It is astonishing that the first traces of Manichaean activity in the Roman Empire—in Syria—date to his lifetime. Shortly thereafter, Manichean communities appeared in almost all the provinces.

This great missionary activity caused concern among the Roman authorities. Manichaeans were a close-knit organization with secretive practices, which made it easy to suspect that they were in the service of a foreign power and involved in spying or sabotage. They were also accused—in those days, such matters were taken completely seriously—of engaging in magic. And thus, when in AD 297, an armed conflict with Persia broke out, drastic repressive measures were launched against them.

However, the persecution did not yield good results. The religion, although suppressed on the surface, survived underground in numerous centers of the Empire.

The Christian writer Eusebius of Caesarea says that Manichaeism was still spreading several years after Diocletian's edict. It is worth quoting Eusebius's words on the matter, as they show an astonishing convergence with the emperor's views:

> In his life, he [Mani] was a rude barbarian. And in his speech and his manners, he was demon-possessed and insane—and so were his intentions. False and ungodly principles stolen from numerous heresies, all equally impious and long since extinguished, poured out of Persia into our countries as if some deadly poison. Henceforth, too, the impious name of the Manichaeans has spread among many people.[19]

---

[19] Eusebius, VII 31

Reading his report, one might think that Diocletian and Christians were allies. And they were, but only against a common enemy. For soon, there was to be an open war between them.

Diocletian and Fortune Tellers

Roman authorities have always punished very severely the practice of magic and astrology. And not because they were fraudulent and superstitious. Quite the opposite. Roman authorities treated these pseudo-sciences with utmost seriousness. They feared that they could harm not only private individuals but also the state—because fortune-tellers and astrologers were able to uncover government secrets and even threaten the lives of rulers. Indeed, the belief in such powers was so firmly established that, from the beginning of its statehood, Rome had maintained its own official diviners, called *haruspices*.

They discerned the will of the gods from various omens and especially from the entrails of sacrificial animals. The *haruspices* had considerable influence on the course of political affairs under both the republic and the empire.

Diocletian, a faithful and practicing follower of the old religion, never skimped on sacrificial animals for the temple altars, while priests and diviners interpreted for him how his gifts had been accepted. During one of these rites, something unusual is said to have happened.

Lactantius writes about it as follows:

Diocletian was in the East. His cowardice drove him to worry about the future, so he offered animal sacrifices to the gods. In their livers, he studied what Fate was preparing for him. However, some among his servants already knew our Lord [Jesus Christ]. These, assisting at the sacrifice, made the immortal sign [of the cross]on their foreheads. It caused the evil spirits to flee and the sacrifice to fail. Terrified *haruspices* could not discern any message in the entrails. They repeated the sacrifices many times as if the previous ones hadn't been thwarted, but the murdered animals still showed nothing.

Finally, the chief *haruspex*, Tages—whether he noticed something or just suspected it—announced:

"The sacrifices do not yield answers because the service is attended by non-believers!"

Diocletian, raging with anger, ordered that the sacrifices be made not only by the servants but by all the people in the palace, and whoever refused was to be flogged. He also sent letters to officers, demanding that they compel their soldiers to make sacrifices, and whoever disobeyed was to be dismissed from service.[20]

The story gives us an excellent insight into the mentality of the people of that era, for the emperor, the priests, the courtiers, and Lactantius himself were all representatives of what we in Eastern Europe call the *intelligentsia*: educated professionals. The narrative also contains important factual clues.

There is no reason to doubt that the reported event did indeed take place. During the sacrifice, someone misbehaved—people always do—one blew his nose, or fell asleep, or whispered with his neighbor—and someone perhaps indeed genuflected—which the priests noticed and exploited for their own purposes.

They raised the alarm that the sacrifice had been rendered invalid because the enemies of the gods had interfered with it. Now, both sides—bear this in mind!—treated these beliefs with all seriousness. Christians—among them the learned scholar Lactantius—neither denied the existence of the pagan gods nor the ability of pagan priests to discern the future. The only point where they and the pagans differed was this: Christians considered the pagan gods demons and the fortune-tellers evil-doers. And vice versa: the *haruspices* claimed that the presence of Christians had a pernicious influence on the course of the sacrifice. Both groups functioned in the same sphere of business and fought by the same methods. The whole problem boiled down to whose god was better and more potent, for

---

[20] Lactantius, 10

no one denied that they all existed.

Lactantius implies that there were Christians in the emperor's entourage. This is confirmed by other contemporary sources, most notably the *History of the Church* by Eusebius of Caesarea. And since this writer will appear on these pages again, we should take a moment to introduce him.

Eusebius of Caesarea: Concerning Christians

Eusebius was born in Palestine around AD 260, and around 315, he became bishop of Caesarea Maritima, the principal harbor of that province. In later years, he came into contact with Constantine. He died in 340.

Eusebius wrote many religious treatises. The most valuable of these is the above-mentioned *History of the Church,* which records the history of Christianity from its beginnings through Constantine's final victory. Eusebius may have begun his work before 303; in the next dozen years or so, he often had to rewrite it since turbulent times placed facts and personalities in an ever-changing light.

At the beginning of Book VIII, in which he depicts the reign of Diocletian, Eusebius says that it would be a "task beyond his strength" to describe how brilliantly Christianity developed in the years preceding Diocletian and what respect and freedom it enjoyed among both Hellenes and barbarians. He continues:

> And the emperors favored us. They entrusted us with offices, even governorships of whole provinces. And, out of benevolent regard for our religion, they exempted us from the obligation to offer sacrifices. And what about the palace courtiers? The emperors allowed them, their wives, children, and servants to act openly and freely in matters of religion in word and deed: they gave them ample opportunity to profess and proselytize their faith. They even

showed them preferment.[21]

There is probably a bit of exaggeration in these words, but it is indeed possible to point to Christians who held high offices both under Diocletian and under earlier emperors. By that time, the new religion had already spread throughout all the provinces of the Empire and was especially strong in the East. One important reason for its flourishing was the official tolerance Christianity had enjoyed since AD 260, when, with the fall of Emperor Valerian, the last persecution ended. And even that persecution, like all the previous repressions—and contrary to Christian hagiography, they happened rather rarely—had a local rather than universal character, though, of course, the Roman authorities observed the activities of all these strange Eastern religions with suspicion and generally made great difficulties for them.

However, this reluctance was not aroused by their doctrines but by the fact that they often adopted the form of semi-secret organizations whose networks spread across the Empire; and had the most supporters among the volatile poor. Members of these communities often behaved haughtily towards the officialdom. They did not accept its ultimate authority, considering the current social order and state apparatus as evil, and they tolerated them only on the assumption that they were doomed to imminent destruction anyway.

Christians, in particular, proclaimed that they were not subjects of the emperor but of the Messiah, whose kingdom was about to come at any moment and overthrow all earthly government. They categorically refused to offer sacrifices to the images of the emperor. They often evaded service in the army. They mocked the deities and rituals of the official cults, which, in the eyes of the officials, constituted the symbolic bond of the Empire.

For all these reasons, suspicions inevitably arose that Christians were a subversive organization, threatening the established order, tradition, and even the very existence of the Empire. In brief, many officials feared that the Church constituted a state within the state. Also, friction of an administrative nature arose in daily life. Since

---

[21] Eusebius, VIII 1

Christian communities had never received official recognition, their legal status was not defined, which had many consequences, especially when it came to holding public meetings, ownership of property, and the privileges of the clergy.

For all this, major changes in the relationship between Christianity and the state took place in the third century. First, Christianity itself changed in response to the rapid increase of its followers, especially in the cities. Christianity had had an urban character from the very beginning, and already, the first missionaries chose large cities as their center of activity, especially those with large concentrations of Greek speakers. Thus, in many lands of the Empire, mainly in the West, the countryside remained almost entirely pagan—and did still centuries later. This fact is reflected in the origin of the word "pagan," which comes from the Latin term *paganus*, meaning "a villager."

The social base of Christianity consisted of the poor and middle-income strata of the urban population: artisans and small merchants, lower officials, and servants in the great houses. The churches tried to gain at least some sympathizers among the upper classes, yet, in the first centuries, such ties, let alone conversions, were rare. Educated, wealthy people, attached to their traditions, looked with undisguised contempt at the oriental religion, which spread among the plebs and fanatically rejected almost all the achievements of civilization. For early Christianity treated the greatest achievements of literature and art as the work of demons, or at best, as mere playthings that distracted the soul from its true calling. But by the third century, Christians were no longer so uncompromising. They acquired quite a few literate and educated people among their ranks, and it even happened that a Christian might hold a responsible municipal or state office.

Thus, in the forty years since the time of Valerian, there was a mutual rapprochement between the new religion and the secular authorities. Although formally nothing changed, Christianity enjoyed almost complete freedom. The "catacomb period"—when Christianity was largely practiced in secret—had long since passed.

The catacombs in the vicinity of Rome were still visited by the faithful, but completely openly, as cemeteries and places of worship.

Eusebius characterizes this period this way:

> The superintendents of each church had great sway with the procurators and governors. And who would be able to describe the immense size of our communities, which were countless, these massive crowds that gathered in every city, this wonderful influx of multitudes into our houses of prayer? And since it was difficult to fit in old buildings, spacious churches were erected from scratch in all cities.[22]

A curious thing: this great institution did not have a unified and centrally directed organization. Individual communities had total autonomy. They were headed by bishops, *episkopoi* ("overseers"), elected by the faithful to hold spiritual and earthly jurisdiction over them. There did exist, however, here and there, conventions of bishops of one or several provinces, and the authority of certain metropolises was enormous. Alexandria and Antioch prevailed in the east, while Rome and Carthage prevailed in the west. But none of these capitals held absolute primacy. And it was precisely the lack of a central command center that made it possible for a flexible network of independent Christian communes to emerge victorious from all its trials.

This was the case in the past and was about to be again under Diocletian.

The Council in Nicomedia

According to Lactantius, Diocletian's first outburst of anger was limited to the emperor ordering all courtiers and soldiers to make offerings at the altars of the gods. Soon after giving the order, the ruler left for his favorite seat, Nicomedia. He spent the winter 302-303 there.

---

[22] Ibid.

And now Galerius arrived in Nicomedia, supposedly already with the intention of persuading the First Augustus to crack down on Christians. It was said—or at least this is what Lactantius maintains—that Galerius, in turn, was egged on by his mother, the aforementioned Romula. She was a fervent worshipper of ancient Roman deities who looked after the fields and forests. They constituted a trinity: Sylvanus, Diana, and Liber Pater. Their cult had become widespread in the Danubian provinces, where Galerius' parents had settled while fleeing from the barbarians and where the influence of Christianity was weak. While offering sacrifices to the deities, the emperor's mother often invited her countrymen to feasts at which the flesh of the sacrificial animals was served. Christians, of course, refused to attend, and this became a reason for her enmity.

Throughout the winter of 302-303, the two emperors held secret talks to which no one else was admitted. There was a widespread opinion that the talks concerned the most important affairs of the state. It turned out later—these are still Lactantius' assertions, but probably justified since he had lived in Nicomedia for many years, knew many influential people—and the walls of the imperial palace were famously porous—that the subject of the conference was just one: what policy to adopt toward Christians. It was said that the old ruler firmly resisted his Caesar's ideas. He felt that it would be dangerous to stir up trouble throughout the Empire and cause bloodshed. He thought it would be enough if the religion were forbidden to courtiers and in the army. However, these sober arguments failed to convince Galerius. It was therefore decided to seek the opinion of the highest civilian dignitaries and the military. Some of them expressed the view that it was necessary to break up Christianity because Christians were enemies of the state deities and, thus, of the official cults. Others, though personally of a different opinion, supported this position because they knew that this was the will of Galerius.

For all this, Diocletian refused to give his final approval. He decided to turn first to the gods for advice and sent his *haruspex* to the oracle of Apollo near Miletus. The answer came as expected (of course). Only then did Diocletian make his decision: he was unable to resist the combined forces of Galerius, his friends, and Apollo. Still, he tried to maintain a certain moderation: he ordered that all bloodshed be avoided, though Galerius would have gladly burned alive all those refusing to make sacrifices to the old Roman gods.[23]

The above account by Lactantius is all the more noteworthy because the writer was hostile to Diocletian overall, which he makes clear at every opportunity. Here, however, he strenuously seeks to free the senior Augustus of all responsibility and places all the blame squarely on Galerius's shoulders.

How do we explain his hatred of the latter?

As we said above, Christians were scarce in the Danubian provinces he governed. Therefore, Galerius may have underestimated the consequences of unleashing a persecution of Christianity in the East, where thousands of churches flourished. In turn, Diocletian was probably well aware of the conditions in the East. Thus, it is easy to understand that the emperor hesitated, even though, in principle, he was averse to Christianity, as he was to all religious innovations and all organizations beyond state control. He laid this out openly in the introduction to his edict against the Manichaeans.

We will never know what ultimately tipped the scales in Diocletian's mind. It seems likely that he thought it was necessary to remove everything that threatened ancient Roman traditions and the foundations of the state. Pressure from Galerius drove him to make the decision. For Galerius—a simple man with a mentality typical of the military profession—the matter was clear from the outset: whoever did not offer sacrifices to the immortal gods and did not bow before the majesty of Imperial power was a traitor and deserved the consequences of his obstinacy.

---

[23] Lactantius, 11

Nicomedia, February/March AD 303

At first light on February 23, the prefect of the Praetorians, surrounded by senior officers and treasury officials, appeared in front of the church in Nicomedia. They broke down the gates and burst inside. They searched first for statues and paintings, but, in those days, Christians still went without such objects of worship. Instead, they discovered liturgical books and immediately burned them. The crowd was allowed to loot church property. Soon, crowds gathered, and a general pillage began.

The two rulers watched the action from a distance: the church, built on a hill, was clearly visible from the imperial palace. The two now began to argue whether the building should be burned. Diocletian was concerned that this might cause a fire in the city since the church was surrounded by houses on all sides. The Praetorians were sent in. They marched in in battle array, with axes and swords, and set about their task from several sides at once. In a short time, they dismantled the building.

On the following day—February 24—an imperial edict concerning Christians was posted on the walls of Nicomedia. Its copies reached more distant provinces much later—during March and April. The main provisions, as far as we can reconstruct them from various reports, were as follows:

All church buildings were to be torn down, all scriptures to be handed over to the authorities and burned, and all Christians removed from government posts. People of higher status, the so-called *honestiores*, who chose to remain loyal to their religion were to lose the privileges of their status. No Christian would be allowed to appear in court as a plaintiff, even if personal harm had befallen him.

The edict did not provide for the death penalty for the crime of belonging to a Christian community. The legislators were concerned only with destroying the organization and intimidating its members, not with their physical liquidation. It is true that already on February 24, a Christian was executed in Nicomedia; however, he had committed an act carrying the heaviest punishment in any case, for he had dared to tear an imperial edict from the wall and throw it onto the ground while laughing derisively. Even Lactantius disapproved of his conduct. The punishment was severe: the criminal was burned alive.

At this point, a far more serious incident took place, whose consequences were to prove very dire: a fire broke out in the palace at night. Its cause was never identified, but a rumor immediately arose that Christians had started the fire, hoping to burn the two emperors alive. And indeed, a few palace eunuchs were Christian. Diocletian was not fooled by these accusations—as even Lactantius felt obliged to admit. He began a rigorous investigation. The entire household staff was subjected to torture. Diocletian took part in the interrogations. Despite roasting his servants with fire, adds the malicious Lactantius, Diocletian was unable to establish the truth because he did not torture... Galerius's servants. In his view, they had kindled the fire on Galerius' orders in order to lay the blame on Christians and unleash a bloody persecution.[24]

Fifteen days later, a second fire broke out in the palace. This one, however, was put out in time and did not cause major damage. Also in this case, no perpetrators were found. Although winter was not yet over, Galerius left Nicomedia that same day. He announced that he was leaving for fear of being burned alive.[25] While the true causes of the fire were never discovered, it seems that Lactantius's suspicions of a provocation on the part of Galerius were wrong. Many years later, Constantine, a likely eyewitness of the events and an enemy of Galerius, claimed that the fire had been caused by a lightning strike.

---

[24] The Reichstag fire was an arson attack on the Reichstag building, home of the German parliament in Berlin, on Monday, 27 February 1933, four weeks after Adolf Hitler was sworn in as Chancellor of Germany. Marinus van der Lubbe, a Dutch communist, was the alleged culprit; however, Hitler attributed the fire to Communist agitators in general. He used it as a pretext to claim that Communists were plotting against the German government, and induced President Paul von Hindenburg to issue the Reichstag Fire Decree suspending civil liberties, and pursue a "ruthless confrontation" with the Communists.

[25] Lactantius 11-14, Eusebius VIII 2

The Second and Third Edicts

Diocletian remained in Nicomedia and vented his anger on everyone, in particular those closest to him. He suspected his entire entourage. Even his daughter Valeria and his wife Prisca had to offer public sacrifices to the gods. This was not to say that they were Christians, though they may have shown some sympathy for the persecuted. There were quite a few Christians among the courtiers, however, some very influential at that. These suffered death. Christian clergy who had remained in Nicomedia were arrested and executed. Magistrates set up commissions at all the major temples of the city, and the population had to offer sacrifices in their presence. At the tribunals, all parties to all lawsuits were required to demonstrate pious allegiance to the official cults.

As was the rule in Diocletian times, orders were also sent to the Augustus of the West, Maximian, and to his Caesar, Constantius. The former implemented them strictly, especially in the African provinces. On the other hand, Constantius limited himself to tearing down a few buildings where Christians gathered. Christian apologists later praised him for this lenience as a supposedly tacit supporter of the new religion. However, the real reason for his prudent policy was different: in Gaul and Britain, Christianity did not have as many adherents as in the eastern provinces, so repressive action may have been less visible.

Meanwhile, in the spring of 303, unrest broke out in some districts of Syria, triggered by the failure of the winter crop. But, since there were many Christians there, they were accused of having caused the riots.

Accordingly, a new edict of Diocletian was issued in the spring or early summer of 303. It ordered the imprisonment of all Christian clergy throughout the Empire.

Finally, in the autumn of that year, a third edict announced that all who left Christianity would be freed, while those who refused should be tortured. Although prisons were overcrowded in many districts, the governors welcomed the edict with relief and applied its provisions very liberally. Fear of torture drove many of those imprisoned to cave in, while others were coerced to make appropriate gestures. The authorities tried as much as possible to avoid bloody interrogations and resorted to them in rare cases. However, many Christians welcomed—perhaps even craved—the opportunity for martyrdom—as it was thought to guarantee eternal happiness in the next life. Such fanatics refused to accept even the appearance of a concession.

Eusebius, a witness to the persecution in Palestine, gives examples that reinforce the above claim. Some Christians, he says, were forced to make sacrifices—and then immediately let go, although they did not actually complete the assignment properly. Others were said to have complied, and as long as they did not deny it, they were released. But there were those who, even under torture, refused to bow down to the gods. When these fainted with pain, they were often added to the prisoners who had made the sacrifices.

Given such methods, the number of victims could not have been too great. For example, in Palestine, only twelve were executed between 303 and 305. It is true that the edicts against Christians remained formally in force for eight years, that is, until AD 311. In reality, however, the action was not carried out systematically or with the same intensity throughout this time. There were also important differences between different regions.

To be sure, several hundred people paid with their lives for their beliefs throughout the Empire. They were mostly priests. We should remember, however, that the torture to which they were subjected was prescribed by Roman law for all who spoke out against the state: it was not invented specifically for Christians. And we should bear in mind that the picture we have is very distorted, as we have the accounts of only one side—the persecuted one. For obvious reasons, it wanted to present the suffering of the faithful in the most dramatic colors and multiply the number of martyrs.

What is certain, however, is what follows from various statements by church authors and indirectly from further developments—that the number of faithful who apostatized was enormous, and among them were many bishops. The cases of the bishop of Rome, Marcellinus, and of Peter, bishop of Alexandria, became famous. We will return to this issue later, for the widespread apostasy in the days of persecution created a great moral dilemma among the Christians, which in turn led to schism in some provinces, especially in Africa and Egypt.[26]

Diocletian Falls III

Lactantius, who is our only source for the events in Nicomedia, continues:

> There came in the autumn of 303, the twentieth anniversary of Diocletian's assumption of power [counting, by Roman custom, the year 284 as the first]. The main festivities began in Rome on November 20 and were attended by Diocletian himself. For a whole month thereafter, until December 20, there were games, performances, and entertainment. But it seems that Diocletian did not celebrate too lavishly—not, at any rate, as generously as the people of the capital had expected. The emperor, not very pleased with the mood of the public, left Rome before December 20, even though the winter was harsh, with driving snow and freezing rain.
>
> He celebrated the new year in Ravenna; then, as he had done in all the preceding years, he inspected the Danubian provinces. Fatigued by the journey and the cold, he became ill, slightly but chronically, and was carried in a litter almost the entire way. This is how the summer passed. He returned to Nicomedia already seriously ill.
>
> Nevertheless, he showed up in public to dedicate the circus he had built in the city. This took place a year after the twentieth-anniversary celebrations. He then became so ill that special sacrifices were offered to the gods to preserve his life.
>
> On December 13, a mourning mood prevailed in the palace. Sadness

---

was painted on the faces of senior officials, and a terrified silence hung over the entire city. It was reported in whispers that the emperor had not only died but had already been buried. Unexpectedly, on the next day, news spread that he was alive; the faces of the palace servants and courtiers were again beaming with joy. Some, however, suspected that this was not true, that Diocletian's death was being concealed until the expected arrival of Galerius, for fear that the army might stage a coup and install someone else as Augustus.

However, on March 1, Diocletian appeared in public. He was barely recognizable, so had his prolonged illness wasted him. After that critical day of December 13, he gradually regained his vital powers, but never completely. His mental faculties were shaken; there were moments when he went into a kind of frenzy.[27]

The Question of Succession

A few days later (we are still following Lactantius), Galerius arrived in Nicomedia. He did not come to congratulate his adoptive father on his recovery but—to force him to surrender power. Galerius had already broached the matter with the second Augustus, Maximian, and threatened him with civil war.

He first approached Diocletian in a gentle and friendly manner. He reminded him that he was already old and would soon not have enough strength to direct the affairs of state and that he deserved to rest after twenty years of hard work at the helm. He also cited the example of Emperor Nerva, who—two centuries earlier—had handed over to Trajan. (We should note that if Galerius was indeed speaking of Nerva, the allusion was completely unfounded: Nerva had never formally abdicated; he only adopted Trajan and appointed him co-ruler).

To these arguments, Diocletian replied:

---

[27] Lactantius 17

"It is not befitting for me to step back into the anonymity of ordinary life again after climbing to such heights of splendor. Nor would it be safe to do so because while holding power for so long, I made many enemies. As for Nerva, he only reigned for a year. He could not bear the burden of power and responsibility, so he abandoned the helm of state and returned to private life. But if you want the title of Augustus, nothing prevents me from bestowing it on all four of you."

Galerius, who in his dreams had already seen himself as the master of the whole world, understood that he would gain nothing from such a "solution." He, therefore, put the matter more clearly:

"It should be considered an unbreakable rule that the empire will always have two higher dignitaries in charge of the whole empire and two lower ones, aiding them in the exercise of power, for two equals will always easily agree and compromise, while four will never do so. If you don't want to step down, I will think of a solution so that I no longer remain at the lower rank. After all, it has already been fifteen years since I had been exiled to Illyria on the banks of the Danube! I have been battling barbarians while the three of you peacefully rule over lands far more extensive and calmer."

Diocletian had already received letters from Maximian informing him of his talks with Galerius. He also knew that the Danube troops had recently been significantly reinforced. He was helpless. Thus, upon hearing these words, he said with tears in his eyes:

"Let it happen, then, if you care so much about it."

One more important matter remained: the next two Caesars had to be selected. Diocletian believed that the nominations should be made with the common consent of all the tetrarchs. However, Galerius objected:

"What is the point of this common consent of four if those two in the West, as they are the lower-ranking pair, have to accept everything we decide here?"

Diocletian assumed that Galerius planned for the son of Constantius and the son of Maximian to become Caesars. In such case, the order would have been as follows: there would have been two Augustuses—Galerius and Constantius, and two Caesars—

Maxentius, son of Maximian, and Constantine, son of Constantius. However, to the old man's surprise, Galerius had a different plan. He loathed the young Maxentius.

He said that the man was mischievous and perverse, proud and arrogant, and allowed himself to disregard the sacred protocol of court ceremonial since he never performed an act of adoration either towards his father or himself, Galerius, which was required even of the closest members of the family. (Maxentius was Galerius's son-in-law, but the affinity did not seem to make any difference).

Galerius had a different kind of objection to Constantine, who enjoyed widespread popularity at court, where he had been staying for at least eight years in the capacity of an honored hostage. He had grown up to be a very handsome young man: tall, erect, with expressive features.

He distinguished himself by his bravery in several campaigns, over the Danube and in Asia, and earned a great deal of respect among the soldiers. Diocletian appointed him a tribune of the first rank—a high dignity, an office often held by emperors in the past. He also sat on the imperial council. Things were not as good with his general education, especially with his knowledge of literature, which was then considered the most important subject of study. Constantine had also not studied the principles of Roman law, although this skill would have been of great use to a future ruler. Nevertheless, over time, as emperor, he developed a dynamic legislative program and broadened his interests to include the field of philosophy.

But it was Constantine's popularity that worried Galerius: he wanted the future Caesars to be entirely dependent on him. So he proposed that a certain Severus, already an old man, a good officer, but also known for his fondness for wine, should become the Caesar of the West. In the East, on the other hand, this dignity would be assumed by a young Maximinus Daza, a relative of Galerius, also an officer.[28]

According to Lactantius, such was the course and outcome of the dramatic talks between the ailing Diocletian and his Caesar, the

---

[28] Lactantius 18

brutal and implacable Galerius. They took place in March or April 305 in Nicomedia. Of course, we could doubt the veracity of this account. After all, by what means did the professor of rhetoric, and moreover, as a Christian, most certainly in disfavor at the time, manage to see the minutes of the secret conference? Lactantius undoubtedly only repeats what was said in the city about the confrontation between Diocletian and Galerius. This was how his contemporaries imagined the discussions of the two rulers.

It was widely believed that Diocletian was reluctant to abdicate but was forced to do so by Galerius, eager to assume the first place in the empire. Galerius also forced him to approve both future Caesars, Severus and Maximian Daza, and managed to get the Augustus of the West, Maximian, to resign.

We do not have any official records to indicate what Diocletian's intentions were in stepping down from the throne and whom he would have liked to see as the new Caesars. Hence, among modern scholars, opinions are divided. The prevailing opinion is that Diocletian had had to resign due to his advanced age and frail health. Who knows whether he had not conceived of it during his illness? In any case, we know that during his stay in Rome at the end of 303, he forced Maximian to swear that he, too, would lay down the purple if he, Diocletian, did so as well. Lactantius, however, may have been right when he highlighted the special role of Galerius in the process. His insistence probably hastened the final decision, and the two new Caesars were, it seems, really chosen by him.

Nicomedia, May 1, AD 305

A vast crowd gathered in Nicomedia. Standing in orderly ranks were not only the troops of the palace guard but also officer delegations of all the legions of the Empire, sent in by their units. The ceremony took place outside the city, on a hill that rose above the plain about three miles away from the walls. Years ago, Galerius had received Caesar's purple from the hands of Diocletian there. The two emperors commemorated that event with a column bearing a statue of Jupiter.

And now a procession headed toward the hill. Old custom required that a soldier's rally be held during an imperial acclamation. In front of the troops and the legionary insignia, the two rulers stood on the podium. All eyes, says Lactantius, were on Constantine, and all rejoiced in advance at the thought that he would be appointed Caesar. In the secrecy of their hearts, they offered him their best wishes.

Diocletian took the pulpit. He spoke with tears in his eyes. He stated that he was ill and needed respite after so many hardships. Therefore, he wished to transfer power to younger hands and appointed new Caesars. The crowds of thousands waited in the greatest suspense to hear what names would follow. But Diocletian unexpectedly mentioned Severus and Maximian.

The crowd, says Lactantius, was stunned. High up, on the tribune, stood Constantine. They asked in whispers: perhaps there was a mistake? Then Galerius reached behind him and pushed forward Maximinus Daza. He ignored Constantine and took off his cloak from Daza's shoulders in order to clothe him in purple.

Everyone strained their eyes in shock: what man was this? Where had he come from? However, no one dared to protest. And then, Diocletian took off his purple cloak and threw it on Galerius's shoulders. He thus became a private man again, a mere mortal, Diocles.

And that was the end of that unusual ceremony. They were already returning to the city. The recent lord of the empire rode out of the city on an ordinary Galician cart; he headed for his homeland, Dalmatia. "And a man who once shepherded cows," says Lactantius, "and then rapidly ascended the military ranks, took over the provinces of the East."[29]

This is the main thrust of Lactantius' account of an event to which he probably was an eyewitness. It is obviously biased and was written with undisguised passion. Resentment against Diocletian,

---

[29] Lactantius 19

hatred for Galerius, contempt for Maximinus Daza, and attachment to the wronged Constantine imbue every sentence. We should also remember that Lactantius wrote his work at least twelve years later, already closely associated with Constantine as his sons' tutor. This naturally raises a suspicion that the account is not credible. Yet, not only the description of the ceremony itself but also of the reaction of the audience is probably true. After all, it is understandable that the general public was expecting the appointment of Constantine: it seemed almost certain, given his father's position.

For Constantius now became Augustus. On the same day, May 1, a ceremony faithfully corresponding to that of Nicomedia was held in Milan, in Italy. Maximian handed over the Augustan purple to Constantius, who in turn appointed Severus as his Caesar. In his speech, Diocletian informed the rally in Nicomedia of all this.

On the other hand, contrary to the claims of Lactantius, Diocletian did not become a mere mortal after laying down his purple. He was still surrounded by a nimbus of majesty and still retained great personal authority. He now settled permanently in his magnificent palace near Solin. (He had been building it for a long time). Reportedly, his main occupation became the growing of cabbages in the palace garden. Who knows whether, in this way, he did not try to forget about the developments threatening his political system erected with such strenuousness over twenty years. For soon, events took place that made it obvious that the Empire would once again plunge into the abyss of civil wars.

Part Two
FROM YORK TO ROME

The New Tetrarchy

And now a new imperial tetrarchy came into being. The Augustuses were Galerius in the East and Constantius in the West, and their Caesars—Maximinus Daza and Severus, respectively. As had been during the first tetrarchy, the system was cemented by family relationships: the Augustuses adopted their Caesars as their sons. A territorial division of spheres of influence was put in place: Galerius oversaw the Balkans and Asia Minor, while Daia oversaw Syria and Egypt; Constantius governed Britain, Gaul, Spain, and part of present-day Morocco, while Severus held the rest of North Africa, Italy, the Alpine countries, and Pannonia. Of course, as during the first tetrarchy, this was not a formal division of the Imperium. It remained a unified state, at least in theory. A visible symbol of this was that everyone recognized Constantius as the Elder Augustus, that is, as the preeminent ruler. His seniority resulted from having been appointed Caesar on March 1, 293, while Galerius did not arrive until May 23 of the same year. The three-month difference gave Constantius the privilege of first place.

Galerius, though very ambitious, had to accept this. In any case, he expected that Constantius, who was very ill, would soon pass away, and then Galerius would naturally take his place as the senior Augustus. Reportedly, he also considered the possibility of deposing

Constantius from the throne in case the matter dragged on, as he was sure that both Caesars would be loyal to him and not to Constantius.

Galerius had a man at his side, a peer almost, with whom he had been friends since his first years of military service. He was Flavius Licinianus Licinius, commonly called Licinius, and had been Galerius' advisor for years. Galerius planned for him to become the Augustus of the West in place of Constantius. Then, Galerius would lay down the reins of power, probably about 312, after solemn celebrations of the twentieth anniversary of his reign (counting from the year 293), and appoint his own son, Candidianus, as Caesar. The boy would be seventeen years old by then.

There was no place in any of his for Constantine. He continued to play the role of an honored hostage. He stayed at the court of Galerius, guaranteeing his father's loyalty by his presence.

The Reign of Galerius

If we were to believe Lactantius unreservedly, we would have to conclude that the reign of Galerius was particularly harsh and ruthless, even against the background of an era that knew so much evil and cruelty. Here, in abbreviated form, is part of Lactantius' report about this ruler's reign:

> All criminals, real or alleged, were punished as severely as possible. The use, formerly strictly observed, that people belonging to the upper stratum (*honestiores*) were not to be subjected to torture was no longer heeded. Light punishments, such as exile to islands, imprisonment, or forced labor in the mines, were not used at all; people were sentenced to death by burning alive, crucifixion, or by being thrown to wild animals. Galerius himself watched with genuine fondness as the condemned were torn apart by bears, which he kept at his court especially for that purpose. People of lower status, especially Christians, were burned, but only gradually, over many days, starting with the feet and working up. Death by beheading was considered a privilege, graciously granted only to

those who were found in some way deserving.[30]

However, the picture outlined by Lactantius is certainly biased. In the interest of fairness, we should note the brief but eloquent remarks of other ancient authors, if admittedly somewhat later. Eutropius, who lived in the second half of the fourth century, characterized Galerius very kindly: "A man of good manners, excellent in military affairs."[31] Somewhat naive but equally positive was the judgment in a chronicle from the end of the same century:

> Galerius deserves praise, even if his understanding of justice was primitive and rural. He was distinguished by his beautiful demeanor. He was a talented and lucky commander. He came from a peasant family, and in his youth, he grazed flocks [*armenta*] and hence received the nickname *Armentarius*.[32]

It seems that it is possible to reconcile the opinions of these historians with Lactantius. Galerius' primary intention was to strengthen the state, and he persecuted Christians because he saw them as its enemies. Lactantius is perhaps correct in claiming that the emperor modeled his actions on oriental despotism, which he learned during his wars with the Persians, and that he, therefore, treated his subjects like slaves. However, why look so far? Why assume that Galerius needed any examples? His methods of governing were simple and soldierly because that was the mentality of the ruler. He wanted to rule the state as one would command a military camp. He settled all problems of social life briefly and decisively by means of blunt barracks discipline.

The functionaries of Galerius were primarily his officers. Civil offices, especially governorships, were filled with them. Deprived not only of any culture but even of the basic knowledge of civil law, they passed judgments according to their own understanding of order and discipline. They paid no attention to traditional norms nor even to their own prosecutors. Defense attorneys were removed from courtrooms for unnecessarily complicating court proceedings. All

---

[30] Lactantius 21-22

[31] Eutropius X 2

[32] *Epitome de Caesaribus*, 40, 15

intellectual activity was held in suspicion, and its creators were persecuted.

For the broad masses of the population, the most onerous was the great tax census of AD 307. It covered the entire population with all its strata and registered all cultivated land and farm animals. Census officials were, of course, vitally interested in placing as much property as they could in the highest category, as this was the basis for the determination of the amount of tax. A contemporary testimony claimed that they behaved like conquerors in a conquered country. The situation was aggravated by the fact that the authorities did not believe anyone, not even their own officials: a not uncommon thing in any bureaucratically ruled country. Thus, new inspectors, supervisor inspectors, controllers, and super-controllers were sent in again and again. Each new arrival, to justify his salary, strove to find some irregularity in his predecessors's work and ratchet the tax assessments higher. In the end, the only ones left out of the census were the homeless, from whom nothing could be taken away. But a way was found for them as well: they were all herded onto boats, which were sunk on the high seas.

Constantine Slips Away

In the early spring of 306, even before the great tax census discussed above, urgent letters came to Nicomedia from the western reaches of the Empire. The senior Augustus, Constantius, reported that he was seriously ill, and asked that his first-born son, Constantine, come to his bedside as soon as possible.

The ruler of the West had sent similar requests before, but Galerius always dismissed them. For understandable reasons, he preferred not to let a valuable hostage out of his sight. He may even have thought about murdering Constantine, as his death would have removed once and for all any threat from that quarter. He may even have taken some steps in that direction: according to one account, he challenged the young prince to fight a lion in the palace arena, but Constantine, strong and skillful, emerged victorious from the ordeal. There were going to be further similar attempts and some news of this must have reached Constantius, which was why he demanded the return of his son. Since a refusal could have serious political consequences, Galerius had no choice but to agree.

Already at the end of the day, the emperor affixed his seal to an order allowing Constantine to use the state post for his journey. But he instructed the young man to leave only the following day after receiving additional instructions. The next day, the emperor slept a little longer than usual, until noon, and only then summoned Constantine. But the prince was nowhere to be found: he had left the previous evening as Galerius was resting after dinner. The enraged ruler sent out a pursuit.

However, the soldiers soon returned, reporting that upon arriving at the first post station, they had found all the horses dead. As he fled, Constantine changed horses at the posts, killing the ones on which he arrived. The prince had decided to make this daring escape because he had seen through Galerius' plans: while seeming to allow his departure, he was preparing an ambush to kill Constantine as he traveled through the mountainous countryside.

The Death of Constantius

His father met Constantine in a port city of northern Gaul, which is today called Boulogne. A war fleet was just setting sail, for Constantius was preparing an expedition against the Picts, who were still troubling the Roman province of Britain from the territory of present-day Scotland. A born novelist, Lactantius depicts the young man's meeting with his father briefly but dramatically:

> With unbelievable speed, Constantine returned to his father, who was already dying. The latter commended his son to his soldiers and handed power to him. This is how he found on his deathbed the

longed-for rest from a lifetime of toil.[33]

On the other hand, the Greek *Life of Constantine* paints the scene with great pathos. Its authorship was once attributed to Eusebius of Caesarea, though today, many think that this work was written only at the end of the fourth century, by which time Constantine was regarded as the embodiment of all Christian virtues, a man of providence and an ideal ruler. The tone of the work is highly panegyrical, and the actual course of events is heavily redacted. Thus, it is advisable to use this source very carefully and preferably only when no other source is available. The description of Constantius' death perfectly illustrates the nature of the work:

> When the emperor saw that, contrary to his greatest fears, his son now stood next to him, he jumped out of bed, put his arms around him, and called out:
>
> "The soul of a man already departing from this life has been relieved of its only sorrow!"
>
> Then Constantius gave thanks to God and said:
>
> "I now prefer death to immortality."
>
> He gave instructions as to all his affairs. He said farewell to his sons and daughters, who surrounded him in a tight circle like a choir. He died in the imperial palace, on the imperial bed, passing on the inheritance of the empire in accordance with the law of nature to the eldest of his progeny.[34]

In reality, matters looked differently. Constantine did meet his father in Boulogne. Constantius was probably already ill but still capable of leading an expedition against the Picts. He died only after the end of that expedition, in the military camp in Eboracum, or present-day York, on July 25, 306. It is true, however, that the dying Augustus appointed Constantine his successor.

---

[33] Lactantius 24
[34] *The Life of Constantine*, I 21

Caesar Constantine

The official version of the events at Eboracum was that, after his father's death, the army forced the prince to accept the imperial purple. Unknown to us by name, the author of a certain panegyric in honor of Constantine thus wrote about it a few years later:

> Benevolent gods! What good fortune they bestowed on Emperor Constantius at the moment of his death! Departing for heaven, the Emperor saw his heir. And as soon as he was taken from this earth, the entire army unanimously agreed to acclaim you. The hearts and minds of all desired your appointment. And although you wished to leave the matter up to the decision of the senior emperors, the fervor of the soldiers preempted what they soon approved.
>
> As soon as you showed up for the first time, the soldiers, having in mind not your feelings but the good of all, imposed the purple on you, even though you had tears in your eyes. But you resisted them for it is not befitting for a sanctified ruler to cry. It is also said, O Invincible Commander, that you attempted to flee from the insistence of your own army; you spurred your horse. You must now hear a word of truth: in doing so, you erred, but that was due to your young age.[35]

It seems that the scene had been staged very carefully. Constantine allegedly attempted to refuse the dignity, but the soldiers imposed it upon him by force. The theater was easy to arrange, for those who had fought under his father's orders for years considered it only natural that the successor of the late Augustus should be his eldest son.

Of course, this act amounted to a violation of the order of the tetrarchy. After the death of Constantius, Galerius became the senior Augustus, while Severus became the younger: they should have appointed the new Caesar. Meanwhile, the soldiers in Eboracum hailed Constantine not even as Caesar but as Augustus!

In essence, this was a relapse into the dangerous practices of

---

[35] Panegyric VII 8

the third century, when individual armies elevated their commanders to the purple as they saw fit. Therefore, official propaganda later emphasized that Constantine had not wanted power and had preferred to leave the matter to the legitimate lords of the Empire.

As it was, they faced a *fait accompli*. Constantine's envoys to Galerius carried letters and an effigy of the new Augustus adorned with laurels; its acceptance would have been tantamount to accepting everything that had happened in Britain.

Galerius pondered what to do. In his first fit of fury, he reportedly wanted to burn the effigy of the self-proclaimed Agustus and do the same with his envoys, for he had had completely different plans for arranging the affairs of the Empire. However, his advisors dissuaded him from such an act; they pointed out that refusing to recognize Constantine would amount to a civil war, while the army of Britain and Gaul was among the strongest. In the end, Galerius, with great reluctance, accepted the image and, for his part, sent the purple cloak to Constantine—but not that of Augustus, but of Caesar. Thus, the two made an honorable compromise: Constantine held on to power but only in fourth place in the system of the tetrarchy, after Augustus Galerius, Augustus Severus, and Caesar Maximinus Daza. Galerius, on the other hand, showed that he was the ultimate source of legitimacy.

The dangerous consequences of this concession were soon to manifest themselves.

That Maxentius Fellow

The issue boiled down to the following question: if, in one case, the right to inherit the throne was recognized, then on what basis was the same right denied to someone else?

Constantine was not the only son of an Augustus. Rome was home to Maxentius, son of Maximianus, the Augustus who, against his will, had been forced to lay down his purpurle simultaneously with

Diocletian in 305. Maxentius was not made Caesar at the time because he had alienated Galerius. The young man, of course, felt the humiliation very painfully and was only waiting for a chance to seize power. The fact that Constantine succeeded only encouraged him.

The opportunity came in the autumn of 306 when Galerius made two mistakes. First, he decided to tax the people of Rome, who had been free from all state burdens since time immemorial: after all, they, the Romans, were still the masters of the Empire, the rulers of all the conquered lands and peoples. The arrival of the census officials caused an unheard-of outcry.

Galerius's second mistake was his decision to disband the Praetorian Guard, which had been stationed since the beginning of the empire in Italy. The decision was correct insofar as the Praetorians were no longer needed as a military force since the rulers resided in other cities of the Empire: even Severus resided in northern Italy, in Milan and Aquileia. However, the Praetorians, who were living well and peacefully, were not going to accept the order of the First Augustus.

Riots broke out. Imperial tax officials were murdered. It is impossible to determine today—because our sources disagree—who started the ball rolling: was it Maxentius who exploited the mood of the populace and the Praetorians, provoking the incidents through his agents? Or, on the contrary, did he only appear on the scene once blood had been spilled and the crowd was casting about for a leader? One way or another, on October 28, 306, Maxentius donned the purple. He undoubtedly thought that Galerius would relent again and make him Caesar to avoid war and preserve a semblance of legitimacy. Maxentius had every reason to expect such a turn of events. After all, how was his situation different from Constantine's? He, too, had taken power as a result of a spontaneous public acclamation. Maxentius's hopes were also bolstered by the fact that he was Galerius's son-in-law.

However, Galerius could not accept a fifth co-ruler. So he instructed Severus, then residing in Milan, to put down the Roman uprising. And there, he made his second mistake. He underestimated the determination of the populace, ready to defend to the end the ruler they elevated. He also failed to take into account that Severus's army consisted of troops that had been under the orders of the father of Maxentius only a year earlier.

Meanwhile, the usurper very skillfully exploited these circumstances. He invited Maximian, his father, to the capital and made him Augustus for the second time. When Severus approached the walls of Rome with his army, his own soldiers deserted him and went over to the side of their former commander. The rightful ruler retreated with the remnants of his troops to Ravenna, a well-defended and well-provisioned city.

He hoped that Galerius would soon come to his relief. But winter had set in, and the Alps became impassable. Fearing that his soldiers would not be able to withstand a prolonged siege and would surrender to the enemy, Severus entered into negotiations with Maxentius and Maximianus. He capitulated on only one condition: that they spare his life. Thus, the recent lord of the western part of the Empire was taken to Rome and interned in its suburbs. He died in 307. Some sources claim that he was hanged on the orders of Maxentius, others that, by way of mercy, he was allowed to open his veins.

Because the victorious Maxentius had effectively deposed Severus, the empire now had three Augustuses—Galerius, Maxentius, and Maximian (for the second time); and two Caesars: Maximianus Daza and Constantine.

Constantine and the Franks

During these events, Constantine was busy on the Rhine.

The Franks, who had been harassing Gaul for so many years, tried to exploit the British expedition and then the death of Constantius. They expected that—as had happened so many times before—a change on the throne would cause unrest in the Empire and weaken the defense of the border. But the young ruler crossed over from Britain to Gaul soon after the York ceremony and immediately went into action. He broke up two invading armies that had crossed the river and captured two Germanic kings; he ordered both to be put to death.

We know little about the battles that took place in 306 and early 307, for they are only vaguely reported in the usually verbose eulogies in honor of Constantine delivered in later years. Relatively speaking, the panegyric of the year 310 presents the events most clearly. The speaker admits that the emperor dealt with both kings harshly but exclaims:

"Let your enemies hate you as long as they fear you!"

The speaker further assures us that the victory made the Rhine border completely secure while previously, the Germans had crossed it whenever they liked, whether when the water was low in summer or when it froze in winter. He states proudly:

> Now, our forts on the river only decorate it because they no longer have to defend it. An unarmed farmer cultivates the shore that once inspired such terror; our flocks bathe freely in the river.

A little later, Constantine crossed the Rhine and ravaged the lands of the Bructeri.[36] The invasion was lightning-fast, and the population had no time to take refuge in the forests or among the marshes. The speaker exclaims with elation:

> Countless people were killed, and masses were taken captive. All cattle were either seized or slaughtered. All settlements were burned. The men were too treacherous to be pressed in our military and too proud to work as slaves. They were led into the arena. And there were so many of them that they soon sated even the most bloodthirsty beasts.[37]

In 307, imperial affairs recalled Constantine from the Rhine.

---

[36] In present-day North Rhine-Westphalia. Their territory included both sides of the upper Ems (Latin *Amisia*) and Lippe (Latin *Luppia*).

[37] Panegiryc X 10-12

Fausta

In the spring of 307, Galerius began to take steps against the usurpers Maxentius and Maximian. In the new situation, much depended on what Constantine would do. If he opted for legitimacy and supported Galerius, the Augustuses of Italy, threatened from two sides, could not hold out. His neutrality, on the other hand, would have given them a good chance of survival.

Knowing this, in April, as soon as Galerius' army began to move, Maximian hurried to call on Constantine in Gaul, even though he was more senior than Constantine, both in age and in dignity. The talks between the two rulers probably took place in Trier, which at the time was the capital of the lands beyond the Alps. Constantine had no reason to be fond of Galerius, but common prudence dictated that he should wait to see how events would develop. So, negotiations with Maximian proved long, dragging on for months while everyone listened eagerly for the news from Italy.

Galerius entered Italy and marched straight on Rome. Here, however, he was overawed. He had never seen the capital of the Empire and had realized neither the enormity of the city nor the power of its defenses. The defensive walls, built more than thirty years earlier by Emperor Aurelian and since then constantly reinforced, were more than eighteen kilometers in perimeter; their remains still make a great impression today. Since it was a physical impossibility to enclose such a large circumference with a regular siege, Galerius pulled back from Rome. He set up camp in the city of Interamna, a few dozen kilometers north of the capital. From there, he intended to ravage the area with raids in order to deprive the city of provisions and force Maxentius to capitulate. He chose this tactic also because of the mood among his troops, who betrayed no desire to storm the menacing walls. Galerius's soldiers, although they came from distant lands, were mostly Romans and felt themselves to be Romans, and the idea of attacking the cradle of the Empire seemed to them sacrilegious.

Meanwhile, Maximian, in order to secure Constantine's

neutrality, offered him the title of Augustus and the hand of his daughter, Fausta. It seems that the marriage had already been proposed once while Constantius was still alive, shortly after 293. We know this from a mention in a certain panegyric whose author claims that in the banquet hall of the imperial palace in Aquileia, there was a painting depicting a tiny girl, Fausta, giving the boy Constantine a wedding gift almost beyond her strength: a golden helmet, encrusted with jewels and decorated with bird feathers.[38] Later, however, this matrimonial project was abandoned, and Constantine became involved with a girl named Minervina. He lived with her in concubinage, just as his father had once lived with Helena. Around 303, she gave him a son named Crispus.

As news trickled in from Italy, Constantine began to view his guest's proposals more favorably. He had treated him as a legitimate Augustus from the beginning, but now, Galerius's position seemed to get worse by the day. Finally, the invader of Italy understood that he would gain nothing by force and, in early autumn, offered negotiations. But Maxentius had taken advantage of the lull in action to bribe enemy soldiers. The specter of widespread defections terrified Galerius. He began to fear the fate of Severus. He reportedly threw himself at the feet of his soldiers and begged them not to hand him over to his enemies. He ordered a retreat in November. Fearing pursuit, he allowed his men to plunder and destroy everything along the way to make it difficult for a pursuing army to supply itself. And Galerius's men were happy to oblige: they robbed and pillaged as if they were in an enemy country. They raped, tortured, murdered and burned. As a result, the opinion formed in Italy that Galerius was a barbarian, a man of foreign origin who desired the destruction of everything Roman.

In this situation, Constantine did not delay any longer. He accepted Maximian's offer, even though, despite the older man's insistence, he did not move to cut off Galerius's retreat from Italy.

The marriage with Fausta and the elevation of Constantine to

---

[38] Panegyric VI 6

the rank of Augustus were celebrated simultaneously, probably on the same day at the end of 307, almost certainly in Trier. It seems highly likely that December 25 was selected. This would have been a significant date since, from time immemorial, it had been regarded as a holiday of the Sun God, who conquered the powers of darkness on that day and began a new victorious advance of daylight. Constantine was then, and for many years afterward, a fervent follower of the Invincible Sun, just like his father had once been.[39]

A eulogy delivered by a rhetorician during the wedding, full of praise for both Constantine and Maximian—son-in-law and father-in-law—has been preserved.

A Failed Coup in Rome

After returning from Gaul to Italy, Maximian ruled jointly with his son for several months. In theory, both had equal rights and powers. Soon, however, a conflict arose between them. This is understandable and common in any system of co-rulership, even with such close blood ties. In this case, Maximian's excessive ambition and senile irritability also played a role. He could not bear the fact that his son was commonly held in higher esteem than he. This was only natural since officers and officials preferred to pin their hopes not on someone who, for natural reasons, would have to die soon but on a young man who perhaps had a long reign ahead of him. Maxentius was then thirty years old, at most.

Not understanding the mood among his subjects, Maximian made a cardinal error. He thought he could rely entirely on the soldiers who had once served under him and had recently given such clear proof of loyalty by deserting Severus. In April 308, he tried to stage a coup against his own government. If our sources are to be believed, the

---

[39] For the issue of chronology of 307, see J.P. Callu, *Genio Populi Romani,* Paris, 1960, p. 70-79; J. Lauferie, *Dies Imperii Constanti Augusti,* in *Melanges offerts a Andre Piganiol,* paris 1966, p. 796-806

thing played out in a highly dramatic manner.

Maximian called a great rally of the army and the people in the Roman Forum. The pretext was a state-of-the-empire address. And there would be plenty to talk about! Italy was still bleeding from the wounds inflicted by the recent retreat of Galerius. Very concerning news came from Africa, where the vicar of the diocese, Domitius Alexander, had either already donned the purple or was about to do so. We should remember that Africa—today's Tunisia and Algeria—was the main supplier of grain to the capital, meaning that Rome was about to suffer food shortages.

Both Augustuses—father and son—stood on the podium. Maximian had arranged to be the first to speak. He presented in grim colors the enormity of the misfortunes that have befallen the state in recent years. And, after delivering this long tirade, he pointed to his son and called out in a big voice:

"Here is the perpetrator of all this evil! Here is he who has brought all these calamities upon us!"

And at once, with a violent movement, he ripped off the purple cloak from the shoulders of Maxentius. The young man, terrified, in a moment of panic, jumped down from the stand straight into the ranks of his soldiers. Maximian, of course, had expected that hostile shouts against his son would immediately rise from the crowd. How disappointed he was! The soldiers and the people unanimously stood up in defense of Maxentius, and the old man had to flee.

He hastened again beyond the Alps, to Gaul, to his son-in-law Constantine.[40]

The Council of Carnuntum

Maximian was probably hoping for military support from Constantine to overthrow his son by force. But the young ruler of

---

[40] Lactantius 27

Gaul and Britain exercised prudent restraint. He welcomed his father-in-law respectfully but did not make any promises. Blinded by hatred for his son, Maximian did not stop plotting. He came up with the idea of reconciling with his hitherto mortal enemy, Galerius. For this purpose, he went to the Danube provinces, heedless of all risks.

Fortunately for the old man, his plan coincided with Galerius's own intentions. The latter, shaken by the setback of 307, wished to invoke the authority of Diocletian and restore the old order through negotiation. He hoped that the creator of the system of tetrarchy would agree to don the purple again to save his life's work from ruin. At the beginning of November 308, Diocletian, Galerius, and Maximian met at a war camp near Carnuntum. This town was located on the Danube, within the borders of the province of Pannonia, slightly east of Vindobona, or today's Vienna.

During the lengthy deliberations, Diocletian adamantly refused to return to the throne. In the end, it was decided that Licinius would be elevated to the purple as Augustus. He donned the purple on November 11. For the time being, he was to rule only Pannonia, but it was expected that in the future, he would strike Italy and remove Maxentius, who was unanimously declared a usurper. Not a word about Constantine was spoken in Carnuntum, though the very fact that he was not invited to the conference was humiliating. Maximian obtained nothing, not even a prospect for the future, for Italy, after its reconquest, was to become the domain of Licinius. Indeed, Diocletian may once again have induced Maximian to relinquish power.

The conference closed with a ceremony, briefly mentioned in an inscription still preserved on a stone tablet. It reads in translation:

> To the Divine Sun, the Invincible Mithras, the guardian of their power, the Augustuses and the Caesars, Jovian and Herculian, filled with submissive piety, rededicated this temple.[41]

Maximian again returned to Gaul. But it was not the end of his ambitions.

---

[41] H. Dessau, *Inscriptiones Latinae Slectae*, no. 659

One Empire, Six Emperors

The Carnuntum conference changed almost nothing. The empire still had six rulers. Four of them ruled "legitimately,"—meaning that they recognized each other: Augustus Galerius in the Balkan provinces and in Asia Minor; Augustus Licinius in Pannonia and perhaps in the Rhetia (Hungary, Austria, parts of southern Germany); Maximianus Daza in Syria and Egypt; Constantine in Gaul and Britain. But there were also two usurpers: Maxentius, ruler of Italy and Spain, and Domitius Alexander, master of the African provinces.

To make matters worse, Licinius Augustus's obsequiousness had become a source of new conflicts. Maximinus Daza felt aggrieved that he was still only Caesar. He had wanted the title of Augustus. He believed that the elevation of Licinius was illegitimate since he had never served as Caesar. In the west, on the other hand, objections were raised by Constantine, who once again had been demoted from Augustus to Caesar—for the second time in as many years.

Galerius eventually decided to make a formal concession to appease both Caesars: he granted them both, probably still in 309, the title of *Son of Augustus*. But this empty name did not satisfy either of the two Caesars. Both continued to show their anger and made no secret of how offended they felt. Admittedly, our main source for this period, Lactantius, dwells only on Maximinus Daza's ambitions. This is understandable: for Lactantius, Constantine was a paragon of all virtues, a modest and meticulous man. Thus, he remains deliberately silent on many facts that could portray the young ruler in an altogether different light: as an energetic statesman trying to consolidate his position by various means and in no way differing from the other emperors in this respect. In fact, the two—Maximianus Daza and Constantine—served as each other's sounding boards and allies throughout this period.

During 310, Daza took the decisive step. He notified Galerius that the army had acclaimed him as Augustus. Galerius relented. Later that year, he conferred the dignity of Augustus on both him and

Constantine. Thus, four "legitimate" Augustuses reigned in the Empire from then on. However, before Constantine obtained the coveted dignity, he had to face a great and unanticipated danger that threatened the loss of everything—power and perhaps even life.

A Coup in Arelate

Maximian was in Gaul, at the court of Constantine, treated with honor and respect but removed from any role in government. For the first time since he had reassumed the Augustan purple in the autumn of 308, he was once again a private man. This situation only fueled his senile lust for power.

In 309, Constantine set out across the Rhine against the Franks. It is not entirely clear whether they were the first to take up arms or whether Constantine provoked them by building a permanent bridge over the great river near Cologne. The latter supposition seems more likely, for the Franks had been terribly ravaged during Constantine's previous expeditions and probably would not have dared to strike at Rome without cause.

Besides, the emperor, confident of his tactical superiority, led a relatively small army. This was probably just an effort to intimidate the enemy.

Constantine parted ways with Maximian, most probably in Trier. He moved along the Moselle toward the Rhine while his father-in-law headed south. Maximian traveled slowly, taking advantage of the hospitality of the cities, which, on Constantine's orders, received him with pomp and ceremony. Meanwhile, his men seized all food supplies from all the storehouses along the route. It was soon to turn out that this was a very deliberate move.

Finally, the old man reached the city of Arelate, now Arles, near where the Rhone empties into the sea. Here, he staged a coup: he donned the purple and proclaimed himself Augustus for the third time. At the same time, he seized the imperial treasury and sent letters to all military units, urging them to side with him. The core of Constantine's army was at the time standing in regions not too far from Arelate, on the Alpine ridge, probably on guard against a sudden attack by Maxentius. The usurper also spread the rumor that Constantine had died. To win the support of the soldiers, he gave generous gifts of money and promotions. Thanks to these endeavors, he gained so much that some units adopted a wait-and-see posture; only his bodyguard troops recognized the new ruler.

Massilia

The news of these events fell on Constantine like a thunderbolt out of the blue. He immediately ceased operations against the Franks and moved south in a series of forced marches. We have only one source that gives anything like an account of these dramatic moments of 309. It is an official eulogy, delivered before Constantine in Trier, by an unnamed rhetorician about a year after the events, at the end of July 310. So, we are dealing with an officially redacted version of the events.

Here are the relevant chapters of the panegyric in free translation:

> When the soldiers learned of Maximian's heinous crime, they immediately and spontaneously demanded that you give the order to march out. And when you waited for supplies to be assembled along the way, they cried out:

> Why this unnecessary delay? Thanks to your generosity, we already have more than we need anyway!

> Then, they snatched up their weapons and rushed towards the gates of the camp. Without rest, they marched for days from the Rhine to the banks of the Arar [the Saône]. They did not feel the slightest weariness, and their fighting spirit never waivered.

> Each day they got closer to their goal, their eagerness to take vengeance for the injustice done to you grew. They were in such haste that they became upset by what they saw as your overly

concern for their comfort when, in the port of Cabillonum [Chalon], you tried to secure ships because you wanted them to preserve their strength by sailing. The Arar had never seemed so slow to anyone before. As their ships glided silently and the banks retreated backward, the soldiers raised an outcry that they were standing still.

They took to oars and rowed so fast that they overcame what they saw as the sluggishness of the river. And once they overcame the Arrar, they rushed the current of the Rhone. And they found that too slow, too!

But why dwell on it? It must be confessed in all sincerity: you yourself, Emperor, often had to struggle to keep up with your army. With what momentum they went forward! And when it was announced to them that Maximian had already left Arelate and moved to Massilia [Marseilles], they immediately put up sails on their ships and, with the swift wind, overtook not just the current of the Rhine, but even the gusts of the gale. They loved your divinity so much that all they ever thought and said was:

"Were we already there!"

And yet they knew full well that they were on their way to siege a powerfully fortified city!

Massilia, I hear, juts out to sea, and its port is difficult to access because the bay, penetrating inland, has a very narrow entrance. Only a narrow isthmus connects the city to the mainland.

However, neither the height of the walls of Marseilles, nor the great number of towers, nor even the very location of the stronghold would have prevented you from capturing the city at the first blow, if only you had wanted to. The soldiers stormed the entire length of the walls with such fury that they would have broken in at once.

Unfortunately, the prepared ladders proved too short. But they still tried to compensate for the missing length with their own bodies: they stood on the shoulders of those ascending behind them. Some were already grasping the parapet between the blanks with outstretched hands. But your humanity, Constantine, is mindful of its duties even in the midst of battle. You gave the order to retreat.

You postponed the moment of victory. You did this in order to be able to forgive everyone later. For you feared that an enraged soldier might commit acts that your gentleness would not condone.[42]

So much for the panegyric. It is clear from this account that the first assault on Marseilles was unsuccessful, and Constantine had to step back. About what happened then, Lactantius tells us:

> The emperor personally approached the walls of the city. He turned directly to Maximian, who stood high on the battlements. He was careful not to use harsh and hostile words. He asked what Maximian wanted and in what way he had failed him. In response, Maximian began pelting his son-in-law with all manner of abuse. Meanwhile, quite unexpectedly, the city gates were opened behind his back, and Constantine's soldiers were let in. Soon, before the face of the rightful ruler stood the arrested emperor-rebel, the godless father, the perfidious father-in-law. Constantine sternly reproached him for all the crimes he had committed. He ordered the imperial purple to be torn from the man but he spared his life.[43]

The Last Conspiracy and the Death of Maximian

The quoted panegyrist confirms that Constantine dealt with Maximian very leniently. He exclaims:

> We all saw how you spared that man. And yet, if the first assault on Massilia had succeeded, no one would have been able to save him from the sword!

However, he then adds words of great significance:

> Let him then blame himself, who was unable to benefit from your bounty! Who has decided that he is not worthy of life, even though you allowed him to live. You even spared those who did not deserve it. However—forgive my honesty!—you are not omnipotent. The

---

⁴² *Panegyric* VII 18-20
⁴³ Lactantius 29

gods take vengeance for you, even against your will.[44]

To what events does this statement allude to? Lactantius—our only source to speak more extensively about the whole business, gives us the following account:

> After the failed coup, Maximian lost, as a punishment, both the dignity of Augustus and all the honors that had hitherto been shown to him as the emperor's father-in-law. He could not bear this humiliation. He plotted a new betrayal. He persuaded his daughter Fausta to help him; he promised to give her another husband, more worthy than Constantine. He asked only that she leave the bedroom door open and that she send the guards away. Fausta promised to do so—and immediately informed her husband of everything.
>
> And so, an ambush was prepared, thanks to which the criminal was caught red-handed.
>
> One of the eunuchs lay in the emperor's bed. Maximian got up deep in the night. He figured chance favored him. The guards were few and spaced far apart. He told them that he had just had a dream of which he must inform his son-in-law as soon as possible. He entered the bedroom. In the darkness, he stabbed the eunuch, convinced that he was plunging his dagger into the emperor's body—and immediately left, boasting aloud of his crime. Suddenly, the door opened, and Constantine stood in it, surrounded by armed men. The corpse of the murdered man was brought out. The assassin was stunned. He did not say a word. He was allowed to choose the manner of his death. He hung from a noose.[45]

This is how Lactantius tells the story. Other sources mentioning the case are very sketchy. They can be divided into two groups. Some state that Maxentius committed suicide, while others say that he was put to death on Constantine's orders. All unanimously speak of death by hanging, but they are so cursory that it is difficult to contrast them with Lactantius' account.

Even this does not appear to be reliable. Maximian's alleged

---

44 Panegyric VII 20

45 Lactantius 30

attempt on Constantine's life—with the help of his daughter!—gives the impression of a made-up or embellished story, taken from some adventurous romance: the murderer sneaks in at night into the bedroom but kills someone else because his target was warned in time.

A certain story in the third *Book of Maccabees* sounds very similar. It is a Greek work, written probably in the first century B.C., in Egyptian Jewish circles. During the imperial era, it enjoyed a wide readership, especially among Christians, and it seems almost certain that someone took this plot from it. But it probably wasn't Lactantius who decided to rework this Maccabean plot, for he is only following the official version of events.

The truth was probably far more prosaic. The young emperor ordered his father-in-law to be put to death soon after his capture in Massilia. To justify this political assassination, he had it spread about that the old man had made a treacherous assassination attempt but was captured with a bloodied dagger in his hand and—committed suicide.

Constantine tried to deflect responsibility for this death because he was concerned by the reaction of the son of Maximian, the ruler of Italy, Maxentius. In time, rumors arose that Maxentius had cooperated with Constantine to eliminate his unpredictable father but who knows if the source of these rumors was not Constantine's disinformation machinery? Fake news is not a modern invention. One way or another, we know for certain that signs of hostility between Constantine and Maxentius began to appear in the wake of the affair.

Constantine meets Apollo

Germanic tribes across the Rhine were delighted to hear that Constantine had left and gone far south. They were all too happy to believe that a major civil war had broken out in Southern Gaul, and their chiefs decided to seize the opportunity and stage a raid. Spies immediately reported these plans to the Romans. Upon hearing the news, Constantine's forces marched back north. Who knows, perhaps it had been the very existence of the Germanic threat that had obliged him to march against Maximian that fast in the first place. Filled with anxiety, he called upon a deity that his father had worshipped and for which he, too, had a special reverence at the time: Sol Invictus—the Invincible Sun, usually identified with Apollo.

As the emperor hurried north, he received good news: the alarm had been premature: it turned out that the Germanic warriors were not making preparations for a raid *that season*. It was, therefore, necessary to thank Sol Invictus.

To do so, Constantine went out of his way. He went to the temple of an ancient Celtic deity, probably located on the upper Meuse, in today's French Grand Est. That god had become identified with Apollo and was nicknamed Grannus.[46] At the shrine, the emperor had a mystical experience: he saw a vision of the god.

We know this thanks to the orator who had delivered that eulogy in Trier at the end of July 310. The speech was delivered hot on the heels of the events which means that we have before us the official version propagated by the imperial court at the time. Such panegyrics played the role of today's keynote speeches made by leading personalities at conventions. At the time, it was not customary for the rulers to deliver speeches: they chose an orator to act as their mouthpiece—the ancient equivalent of today's press secretary. Of course, the imperial secretariat determined and approved the text of the speech in advance. Thus, the ruler heard only what he himself wanted to hear.

Here are the words of the panegyrist:

----

[46] Grannus (also *Granus, Mogounus,* and *Amarcolitanus*) was a Celtic deity of classical antiquity. He was regularly identified with Apollo as Apollo Grannus and frequently worshipped in conjunction with Sirona, and sometimes with Mars and other deities. One of the god's most famous cult centers was at Aquae Granni (now Aachen, Germany). Aachen means 'water' in Old High German and is related to the Roman name for the town, "Aquae Granni." The town's hot springs with temperatures between 45 °C and 75 °C lay in the somewhat marshy area around Aachen's basin-shaped valley region. Aachen first became a curative center in Hallstatt times.

I believe, Constantine, that you saw your Apollo there, who, together with the goddess of Victory, offered you laurel wreaths of victory. Each wreath bore an inscription, and each inscription promised you a reign of three decades. Thus, you were promised to see more generations of men than it had been granted to the old man of Pylos to see. But why do I use the word *I believe*? For you saw the god, and in his form, you recognized yourself: a god destined to reign over the whole world, as the inspired hymns of the ancient bards say. I believe that this prophecy is only now coming to fruition. For you, Emperor, are like that god: young, graceful, beautiful!

You have honored the magnificent tabernacle [of Grannus] with such votive gifts as put all former offerings to shame.[47]

What the inscription within the laurel looked like can only be guessed at. Perhaps it was a Roman numeral, such as *XXX*, or *T*, the first letter of the Latin word *ter* ("three times") followed by the numeral *X*, which would mean: "three times ten."

If Constantine had indeed reported such a vision in his propaganda—*as a kind of monogram*—it would be particularly interesting because of the later story of his alleged vision of a Christian symbol. Further, the text seems to indicate that Apollo and Victory each offered Constantine a wreath, and each of these wreaths foretold him thirty years of life or one generation. Since the emperor was already more than thirty at the time, if the two predictions were to come to pass, he could have expected to live to be almost a hundred, meaning he would have seen more than three generations of men, while Nestor, the old man of Pylos, had known only three.

This story deserves attention for several reasons. First, it is an indisputable testimony concerning Constantine's religious beliefs at the time. Secondly, it indicates how ambitious his political plans were. The emperor consciously alluded to ancient ideas of The Golden Age that would come when the Sun of Justice and Happiness shone over the earth. (A poetic vision of this bright future was given in the famous

---

47 PanegyricVII 21

fourth eclogue of Vergil; the orator undoubtedly had it in mind when he spoke of the "inspired songs of the bards.") The propaganda of Constantine proclaimed that the happy age was near because the emperor was an incarnation of the god himself, his earthly manifestation. He tried to spread this vision through other means as well, above all through the coins he issued. Many significant inscriptions appeared on Constantine's coins over the years:

Soli Comiti Augusti: to the Sun, Companion of Augustus

Soli Comiti Constantini Augusti: to the Sun, Companion of Constantine Augustus

Soli Invicto Comiti: to the Sun Invincible, (my) Companion.

It is true that similar inscriptions are also found on the coins of other Roman rulers of the period, for the cult of the Sun was indeed widespread. However, only Constantine decorated his coins with the likenesses of both himself *and* the solar deity.

There was another reason why Constantine was particularly strenuous in proclaiming his worship of the Sun-Apollo. This reason was indirectly connected with the fall of Maximian. As we remember, Diocletian, in creating his system of tetrarchy, took the nickname *Jovius* for himself and assigned *Herculius* to Maximian.

Henceforth, all of Maximian's legitimate successors, that is, both Constantius and Constantine, belonged to the divine *Herculian* dynasty. However, recent incidents shook the basis of this lineage; Hercules no longer looked like the winning ticket; and Constantine decided to take a new patron for himself.

He chose the Invincible Sun.

Constantine's New Pedigree

Early in the panegyric, we are given a telling genealogy of the emperor:

> First, I will speak of the divine origin of your lineage. Many may not know it yet, but those who love you do. Through your grandfather, you are linked by kinship with the divine Claudius. He had breathed

a new life into the Empire as it teetered on the edge of a precipice. He destroyed on land and at sea the huge masses of Goths that poured through the straits of the Black Sea and the mouths of the Danube. Oh, if only he could have graced the human race with his presence a little longer! If only he had not prematurely become a companion of the gods![48]

The Claudius in question reigned 268-270, a short time indeed, but he was famous for his energy and his great victory over the Goths, which earned him the epithet *Gothicus*. Like Constantine's father, he had come from the Balkan provinces, and again like Constantine's father, was a zealous follower of Sol Invictus. The kinship between the two rulers is, of course, complete fiction. Even the author of the panegyric must admit that no one has heard of it. It was invented to justify Constantine's right to rule the entire Empire; in the further course of the speech, the panegyrist made this blindingly obvious:

> Among all the Augustuses of today, you alone were born a Caesar. You were made ruler not by some fortuitous consent of the people or a sudden, favorable coincidence. You obtained the empire by birth.[49]

This strenuous insistence on hereditary rights is very telling. In this way, Constantine made plain his superiority over his colleague-emperors and even Diocletian himself, the founder of the system, for none of them could boast such a great ancestral past.

The author of the panegyric came from the city of Augustodunum, today's French Autun, between the Loire and the Saône. He gave his speech in Trier, the emperor's main residence. The orator looked on with undisguised envy at the great work of reconstruction accomplished by Constantine in that city, once so badly damaged in war. New walls, a circus, basilicas, and a forum were erected here, as well as a new imperial palace. The speaker did not fail to express a pious wish that the imperial favor might also rain on Augustodunum. He deftly linked this request to the mention of

---

[48] Ibid., 2
[49] Ibid., 2-3

Apollo:

> Also with us, in Augustodunum, there is a sacred tabernacle of Apollo, his grove, and his spring. Thus, in our land, too, dwells your deity. You will be surprised to know that the springs are hot, although the earth does not breathe fire, and the taste of the water is mineral.

And he rejoiced in advance:

> Led by pious respect for sacred sites, you will not stint on gifts, you will grant privileges, you will rebuild my homeland.[50]

Lest you think the orator prescient, consider that the imperial chancellery had approved his wishes in advance and all the more willingly since Augustodunum had been ravaged in the course of a civil war decades earlier because of its allegiance to Emperor Claudius II, the very man from whom Constantine now traced his descent.

The ruler visited the city in 311, and on his way there, he saw deserted and uncultivated lands; even the extensive vineyards, beautiful from afar, turned out to be old and uncultivated as he approached. The roads were so steep that it was difficult to move carts on them; for this reason, too, the land could not always make requisite deliveries of food in time. At Augustodunum, Constantine was enthusiastically greeted by crowds gathered from all the surrounding countryside.

Despite the poverty, the streets leading to the palace were beautifully decorated; all the colleges of priests and guilds showed up with their banners and signs; statues of local deities came out of the temples. Although there was only one small orchestra, the emperor saw it several times during his entry, for his retinue moved slowly while the musicians ran ahead of them from place to place.

Constantine held talks with the magistrates and representatives of the people. Feeling pity for their difficult situation, he reduced the tribute by seven thousand *capita*, or about a fifth, and he forgave the arrears of the previous five years. Thanks to this, many

---

[50] Ibid., 22

taxpayers who had hitherto been hiding in the forests or had gone into exile returned to their homeland to cultivate their land again. The grateful city changed its official name to *Flavia Aeduorum*; *Flavia* because of the emperor's family name, and *Aeduorum* because it lay in the lands of the former *Aedui*, allies of Julius Caesar.

We learn of all this from a thanks-giving speech delivered before Constantine in Trier in the early spring of 312.[51]

Galerius Takes to Bed

We've stayed with Constantine for a while, and it is time to see what the other emperors have been up to.

In the spring of 310, Galerius became seriously ill. He was staying in the Thracian city of Serdica, today's Sofia, the capital of Bulgaria. One description of his disease comes from Lactantius. He saw it as divine punishment for Galerius's evil deeds, and his words ooze with triumphant and very un-Christian relish. Here is an abbreviated version:

> An abscess developed on his genitals and began to spread. His doctors lanced it, but the wound healed and then opened up again. There was a dangerous hemorrhage, which proved difficult to stop. After more treatments, the wound healed, but a slight movement caused another hemorrhage, even stronger. They managed to stop it again, but the patient was already exhausted. No medications had any effect. Abscesses spread to all nearby parts. The more they lanced them, the more they spread.

> The most famous doctors were summoned, but no human could save him. He turned to the gods. Apollo was implored, and Aesculapius, but when Apollo's prescription was applied, the disease got even worse. He stood at death's door; the entire lower part of his body became festered. His entrails rotted along with his

---

[51] *Panegyric* VIII 5-14

privates, and maggots infested his wounds.

The stench of festering penetrated not just the palace but the entire city. Animals were set to lick away the vermin. The body had lost its shape. Its upper part was completely shriveled, with yellow skin stretched over the bones. The lower part became bloated like a wine sack, and the legs were deformed.

The illness lasted for a whole year.[52]

Another Christian writer contemporary of the events, Eusebius of Caesarea, gives a similar and perhaps even more vivid description:

Suddenly, an abscess formed in the middle of his private parts, and then a purulent fistula inside it. One and the other spread incurable havoc in the depths of his viscera. An innumerable number of maggots swarmed in these wounds, and a corpse-like stench spread from them. His whole body turned into a clump of gelatinous fat, which began to decompose and presented an unbearable sight to those who approached him. Among the doctors, some could not bear the stench at all and died from it; others were executed because they could not cure that enormous lump of flesh for which there was no longer any hope of rescue.[53]

One would look in vain for even a trace of sympathy in the two Christian accounts. But then they were intended as propaganda tools: they were meant to show what punishments awaited anyone who dared to raise his hand against God's chosen people.

The idea is not original, and some of the details of the disease, especially the worms that hatch in the body while the sufferer is still alive, are taken from Jewish writings. In the second book of the Maccabees, we read a similar account about the death of the Syrian king Antiochus, the persecutor of the Jews. But this is not to say that it is unhistorical. It seems that Galerius was indeed the victim of a malignant tumor or abscess and died after terrible suffering. This is confirmed by many sources.

---

[52] Lactantius 33
[53] Eusebius VIII 16

Galerius Decides to Tolerate

On April 30, 311, copies of an imperial edict appeared on the walls of Nicomedia and other cities of the Asian and Balkan provinces. In accordance with the usage of the day, the headline listed all four legitimate Augustuses—Galerius, Licinius, Maximianus Daza, and Constantine—as authors; however, the real author was the first of them. This is unanimously confirmed by all contemporary sources, even those unfriendly to Galerius. In its rough outline, the edict proclaimed as follows:

> Among the ordinances that we continuously issue for the benefit of our subjects and our state was also the following:

> We wanted to heal the body politic in accordance with the spirit of the old Roman usage. We also wanted to make Christians, who had abandoned the religion of their ancestors, return to reason since, for some unknown cause, they became so stubborn and delusional that they did not follow the laws of the ancients but made new laws for themselves at their own whim and discretion and gathered followers in various places. And when we revealed our will that they should return to the faith of their ancestors, many of them were held accountable, and many suffered punishment, yet the largest part persisted in the error of their ways. It has also come to our attention that there were also those who did not worship our gods but did not remain faithful to their god, either.

> We have now reexamined these matters in our boundless charity and in accordance with our custom of showing mercy to our people. And we have decided that it was necessary to take mercy on these people as well. Let them be Christians again, if they so desire, and let them build their meeting places on the condition, however, that they do nothing against the public order. We will send a letter to our governors to indicate how they should proceed, but in accordance with our present authorization, Christians should pray to their god, asking for the good of us all, for the good of the state and for themselves, so that the state will remain unshaken and they will live

The way Christian authors describe it, we might conclude that Galerius's newest edict was simply an act of contrition on the part of the tyrant, who suddenly realized that he was facing death. It's a rational psychological theory, but all indications suggest that Galerius had moderated his attitude to the new religion some years before his illness, and persecutions continued only in the provinces ruled by Maximinus Daza—in Syria and Egypt.

If Eusebius is to be believed, Daza adopted the edict of toleration with utmost reluctance. He communicated its contents to his officials verbally, and then instructed his secretary to send a circular letter to the governors on the matter; all this because he could not bear to revoke his orders himself.

And now numerous prisoners and exiles returned triumphantly to their homelands—Daza had rarely sentenced Christians to death, preferring to sentence them to forced labor in mines and quarries and, at most, to mutilation.

Since the two rulers of the West, Maxentius and Constantine, had followed very liberal policies, the edict of tolerance passed largely unnoticed in their domains.

The Reign of Maximinus Daza

Soon after the publication of the edict—mid-May 311—Galerius died. Licinius was present at the dying man's bedside. The First Augustus entrusted to him the care of his wife Valeria and son Candidianus, born to him by one of his concubines.

Daza, then residing in Syrian Antioch, immediately hurried north. He wanted to prevent Licinius from seizing the provinces of Asia Minor. The moment he arrived in Nicomedia, he canceled the property census that was about to take place in Asia; in this way, of

---

[54] Lactantius 34, Eusebius VIII 17

course, he wished to win over the population and claim his precedence over Licinius.

The latter, who had at first ruled only a part of the Danubian provinces, had now seized all of the Balkans, and it was clear that he was hoping to take over the entire inheritance of Galerius.

The armies of the two emperors now faced each other across the Bosphorus Straits. No clash occurred—perhaps for the simple reason that neither side had a numerical advantage. After a suitable period of grand posturing, the rulers met in person on a ship in the middle of the Bosphorus Strait and agreed on the obvious: each would keep what he had seized. Daza returned south.

He was now master of the entire East: lands where Christianity had relatively the most adherents. Initially, he adhered to the edict of tolerance. He opened prisons, freed people serving hard labor, and allowed Christian services to be held without hindrance. And bishops began to address the moral conundrum posed by Christians—and there were very many—who had renounced their faith during the persecution. But within six months, the emperor returned to his old policy, changing only the forms of oppression.

First, religious gatherings in cemeteries were banned. Then— a very clever trick!—delegations of residents of various cities began arriving at the imperial court, all of them demanding that Christians not be allowed to build churches in their territory. Lactantius and Eusebius suggest that the messengers were only putting themselves forward at the secret behest of the authorities. It may have been the case in some instances, but we should remember that pagans were still a majority in almost all urban centers, and to be sure, they often took the initiative themselves: they made life difficult for the new religion while gaining the favor of the emperor and of their own deities.

Daza also attempted to build a pagan version of the Christian organization, hoping that it might prove as resilient and mutually supportive as the Christian one. In his cities, he appointed chief priests—the equivalent of Christian bishops. They presided over the colleges of priests of various cults and oversaw offerings to the gods. Obviously, they also felt that Christians should not build new churches in their cities. Above them, Daza appointed a high priest in each of the provinces; both ranks were granted the privilege of splendid robes. All this was partly modeled on the system of the Christian hierarchy and partly on the organization and attributes of the Egyptian priests.

Propaganda measures were not neglected, either. A version of the minutes of Christ's trial before Pilate was circulated—perhaps even without the emperor's knowledge. In it, the accused clearly confessed to all the charges against him. The protocol was distributed to all the provinces. Daza instructed that it be made public in every city and village. It also became compulsory school reading; children were required to learn its text by heart.

Other tricks were used. In Damascus, the military commander seized several prostitutes in the market and forced them to sign a statement that they were Christians and that they knew about crimes committed by the followers of their religion and the abominable acts they committed in churches. Copies of these accounts were also distributed to all localities.

But, as before, the death toll was very low, probably no more than a dozen individuals. It did, however, include the highly respected bishop of Alexandria, Peter, and the famous Antiochian scholar, Lucian.[55]

It is understandable that Christian authors paint a portrait of Maximinus Daza in the blackest possible colors. They portray him as a cruel man, a drunkard, a debauchee, a fearful and superstitious man, and a helpless tool in the hands of charlatans and magicians. Of course, identical accusations were leveled against every ruler hostile to Christianity. Unfortunately, we have few testimonies that we could contrast with the unison chorus of ecclesiastical critics. One of them, however, does make some puzzling statements. He admits that Daza had once been a shepherd but immediately adds, "he revered scholarship and literature and was of a calm disposition." It is true, continues the source, that Daza was overly fond of wine; and, what is

---

[55] Eusebius IX 4-6

worse, under its influence, sometimes issued very harsh orders, which he himself later regretted, and for this reason, he instructed his subordinates once and for all to postpone the execution of his orders until he sobered up.[56]

The account is too cursory to form a useful opinion about Maximinus Daza. But a document has survived that is extensive, indisputably authentic, and authoritative because... it features the emperor's own words. In it, the emperor reveals his religious views and his motivation for his anti-Christian policy. This document is beyond all suspicion for the simple reason that it is cited by... Eusebius of Cesarea in his *History of the Church*. In the simplicity of his heart, the bishop did not realize that by quoting it, he was doing a huge favor to the memory of a man he sincerely hated.

The Confession of Faith of Maximinus Daza

The city of Tyre in Phoenicia instituted certain regulations targetting Christians and notified the emperor. Responding, he wrote a long letter in which he welcomed the Tyrian initiative and assured the city elders that he would lavish favors on them in the future. The residents, greatly honored by this, engraved the entire text on a bronze plaque and put it on public display. Other cities did the same.[57] Eusebius, residing in nearby Caesarea, transcribed the letter and translated it—though not very well—from Latin into Greek, and he included extensive excerpts in his work.

In them, the emperor praises Tyrians for their enterprise and piety, then states:

> It is obvious to me that this salutary idea was suggested to you by the gods, by Jupiter himself, the Best, the Greatest, the protector of

---

⁵⁶ Anonima *Epitome de Caesarbius*, 40, 18-19

⁵⁷ See inscription from Aricanda in E. Diehl, *Inscriptiones Latinae Christianae Veteres*, 1 a-b

your fabled city, your gods, your women, your children.

He breathed into your souls a redemptive resolution. He has revealed to you what an excellent, wonderful, and useful thing it is to worship and venerate the immortal gods with due devotion.

For who is so unreasonable and so utterly devoid of logic as not to see what we owe to the gracious care of our gods? The earth does not in vain receive the seed, nor does she defraud the hopes of farmers; the horror of a criminal war can not easily threaten us; the elements of air and fire do not lose their balance, they do not hasten our bodies towards death; the sea, agitated by gusts of uncontrollable winds, does not throw up destructive waves out of the blue; violent storms do not break suddenly and do not unleash sinister tempests without a proper warning; the earth, our host and mother, does not shake in its depths constantly, the mountains do not come crashing down every day.

And yet it is well known that such and even more terrible misfortunes have frequently happened in the past. But all have happened due to the fault of sinful men, men possessed by hallucination or vain stupidity. Error reigned in their souls and defiled the whole earth.

But let them look at our wide fields! Behold, they stand under crop, and the heavy ears of corn are swaying, and the meadows, sprinkled with rain, are joyful with herbs and flowers, and the wind blows sweet and gentle. May we all rejoice that thanks to our piety, our sacred ceremonies, our reverence for our gods, the winds once so violent have quieted. Long may they rest in the serenity of peace. And even more, let us rejoice, us who have abandoned blind insanity and the pathless wilderness. For we have regained the proper understanding of things, just as we have survived violent storms and severe illnesses and can expect to reap only the sweetness of life in the future.[58]

This beautiful prose came from the pen of a literary person. Perhaps not the emperor himself, but the very fact that people of such caliber

---

[58] Eusebius, IX, 7-11

were in the ruler's closest surroundings gives him a very flattering testimony. In light of this document, it seems clear that Daza fought Christianity for two main reasons. First, he was fervently and sincerely attached to his ancestral faith. Secondly, he blamed Christians for the enormity of the misfortunes that had oppressed the Empire for decades—a view shared by many both then and centuries later.

Of all the rulers of this period, only Daza remained faithful to the political testament of the creator of the tetrarchy. And as the current senior Augustus, he became a symbol of the unity of the empire. So it was no coincidence that Valeria, Diocletian's daughter and widow of Galerius, her mother Prisca, and his son Candidian sought refuge with him even though Galerius had asked Licinius to have care of them. Apparently, they did not feel safe at Licinius's side.

Daza decided to exploit the arrival of his guests for political purposes. He engaged his own daughter to Candidian and decided to divorce his wife and marry Valeria. Christian writers claim, of course, that he was motivated by insatiable lust. But in fact, Daza wanted to consolidate his position by marrying the daughter of Diocletian, the restorer of the empire. Alas, Valeria categorically refused. She offered the excuse that the usual period of mourning had not yet passed (this must have taken place in AD 311). In truth, she refused the marriage precisely because of its politics.

If Lactantius is to be believed, the offended ruler reacted very harshly. He confiscated Valeria's property, banished her from court, tortured her eunuchs, and sentenced several to death. She herself was exiled with her daughter to a desert region of Syria, where she was obliged to move from place to place.

Nevertheless, she managed to inform Diocletian of her fate. The old man begged Daza to send them back. In vain.[59]

---

[59] Lactantius 39-41

AD 312 in the East

Winter rainfall was very sparse, and the year 312 was off to a bad start in Daza's domains. A crop failure came, followed by a terrible famine. As often happens in famine, a plague struck: a fever accompanied by a hitherto unknown ulcer disease, attacking chiefly the eyes, which caused many to lose sight. Thousands of people were dying in the cities, and many villages became deserted; in some localities, the entire tax roster had to be canceled because the taxpayers had disappeared.

Emaciated people were dying in the streets, begging for a crumb of bread. They ate grass. Corpses lay unburied for days because there was no one to collect them. They were devoured by dogs, and the dogs were killed for fear of rabies. Funeral processions were everywhere, accompanied by the plaintive sound of flutes.[60]

Eusebius, for he is the source of these descriptions, dwells with perceptible fondness on the horror of those days. Why, he openly tells us that these calamities were the result of heaven's displeasure with Daza's boastful words in his letter to the Tyrians. This makes us wonder whether Eusebius did not exaggerate in his description of the events of 312, especially since he mentions in passing that Daza simultaneously waged war against the Armenians. This probably meant an expedition to the upper Tigris, where the local Armenian population had become Roman subjects during the last Persian war. These operations proved successful, so the supposedly terrible famine and pestilence somehow did not affect the army. It is likely that Daza also carried out a fundamental administrative reform in Egypt during this time to improve the collection of tribute. The emperor, therefore, acted energetically in different fields and in very far-flung territories, but all the while, he kept an eye on the developments in the West.

It would probably have been simplest and best for the good of the empire—and for the four Augutuses—to accept the status quo, which, in fact, coincided with Diocletian's scheme of the tetrarchy.

---

[60] Eusebius IX 8

Yet, the tetrarchs looked at each other with growing suspicion, and relations between them were more akin to those of hostile superpowers. Eusebius, an eyewitness to the events, depicts it with his usual verve:

> The sea became a dangerous way to travel because those who arrived anywhere by ship had to expect that they might be arrested, interrogated, perhaps subjected to torture, perhaps have their bellies torn open to determine whether they were not, by any chance, spies or enemy agents, and might well be crucified or burned at the stake. Shields, armor, swords and spears, and all sorts of military equipment were forged everywhere; triremes and weapons needed for sea battles were readied. One thought of nothing else but that the enemy may invade any day.[61]

The most tense were the relations between Constantine and Maxentius. And since the former of them clearly made nice with Licinius, Daza, in turn, sought a rapprochement with Maxentius, the ruler of Italy.

The Reign of Maxentius

Constantine's official propaganda, repeated in unison by later Christian literature, portrayed Maxentius as a bloody tyrant and debauched degenerate. However, a different picture emerges if we set aside the usual slanders showered invariably upon all overthrown emperors after their deaths, for it seems that while Maxentius was not without flaws, he certainly did not rule worse or more harshly than his colleagues. Some sources indicate that he took his duties very seriously.

Alas, he had no military talents and no understanding of military affairs. Unlike most of the Senatorial and equite class, he had never served in the army. He rarely took part in army exercises. Indeed, he was not at all eager to leave his palace: it was said that a walk in the

---

[61] Eusebius VIII 15

palace gardens counted as a significant expedition for him. He almost never left Rome, while the capital on the Tiber had not seen an emperor for decades—not even Maximian.

On the other hand, Maxentius, who had been raised in Rome and elevated to the throne by the *Populus Romanus* ("the Roman People"), insisted that the capital of the Empire was still there. He said proudly:

"My Augustan colleagues guard the borders of our empire in our defense."

He also consciously appealed to ancient traditions. He particularly worshipped the god Mars, the forefather of all Romans, and the founder of the city, Romulus. He spared no effort to renovate the capital. In the Roman Forum, he erected a huge basilica named for him. This gigantic building was striking for its innovative vaulting and arches. Its remains still impress today. During the Renaissance, the architecture of this basilica served as a model for the builders of St. Peter's in the Vatican. Maxentius also carried out a major restoration of the great temple of Venus and Roma near the Colosseum. Outside the city walls, on Via Appia, he built a large circus, and near it, he erected a magnificent tomb for his prematurely deceased son Romulus and a beautiful villa for himself.

These construction projects served mainly representational purposes but created employment for thousands of city residents. The emperor's concern for the construction and maintenance of roads was particularly important to the ordinary people. It is safe to say that he cared about matters of communication like probably no one else in his lifetime. The name of Maxentius figures on many mileposts in Sardinia and the African provinces, even though he ruled them for a very short time.

At first, Maxentius enjoyed great popularity. The people of Rome had not only made him emperor but had twice risen in his defense, repelling first the armies of Severus and later those of Galerius. If, over time, the emperor lost this support, it happened not because of some tyrannical antics, as the Christian propaganda sources claim, but under the influence of factors entirely beyond his control. In Italy, it seems, these were years of crop failure, and the usurper Domitius Alexander interfered with food deliveries from Africa, which had supplied the capital with grain for centuries. The consequences were dangerous: prolonged food shortages and high prices.

Naturally, the masses blamed the ruler. Demonstrations led to bloody clashes between the Roman populace and the Praetorian guard. Six thousand were reportedly killed. Only the emperor's personal intervention stopped the fighting, but the hatred for the "tyrant" remained.

Concerning Christians, Maxentius pursued a policy that was not just tolerant but outright friendly. This resulted from the political situation: since Galerius refused to recognize him and at the same time persecuted Christians, he was the common enemy of both, and as the old adage has it, "the enemy of my enemy is my friend." Therefore, the master of Rome, although personally attached to the old gods, quite openly favored the new religion. Not only did he allow adherence to Christianity, but he even restored to Christian communities properties that had been confiscated from them. Unfortunately, the affairs of the Christian community in Rome were terribly complicated, and the emperor had to intervene because a serious concern arose that disputes among the followers of Christ might lead to widespread riots.

In AD 304, Bishop Marcellinus, who had apostatized during the Diocletian persecution, died. He had not only turned the scriptures over to the authorities but even offered sacrifices to the gods. His example was followed by many. Unsurprisingly, when the persecution stopped, the community divided into two camps. The rigorists—led by Marcellus, who was elected bishop in 307—advocated the outright exclusion of those who had apostatized, while the majority of the clergy and faithful favored forbearance. Strong feelings on both sides led to brawls and bloodshed. The emperor removed Marcellus and, shortly thereafter, his successor, Eusebius. Both had to leave the capital. Only Miltiades, elected bishop in 311, mastered the situation.

New Alliances

And now, Constantine went on the attack. He was driven by a cold political calculation. Maxentius seemed easy prey: his troops could not compare with the northern legions in terms of size or combat value; famine was raging in Italy; and there were bloody riots in Rome. Equally important, Maxentius had no allies. Meanwhile, Constantine had already concluded an agreement with Licinius; he engaged his own half-sister, Constance, to him, and her brother, Dalmatius, accepted a high position in Licinius' army.

The two emperors probably intended to share the Empire: Constantine would take the West, while Licinius would take the East. There is also a conjecture that Constantine established secret contacts with the usurper Domitius Alexander, who controlled the African provinces.

But Maxentius managed to regain Africa. This happened in 309 or 310. Alas, he also lost the Spanish provinces to Constantine as early as 311.

Realizing his isolation, he approached Maximinus Daza, who had watched the formation of the coalition of Constantine and Licinius with great concern. Angered by the loss of Spain and emboldened by the support of Daza, the ruler of Italy began to act more boldly. He ordered the statues of Constantine to be toppled and his name erased from all inscriptions. (Until then, the effigies of the other Augustuses had been displayed and venerated in Maxentius's domains because he had wished to emphasize his acceptance of the principle of tetrarchy, even though the other tetrarchs did not recognize him). The circumstances of Maximian's death provided a convenient pretext for Maxentius to attack Constantine. (As you recall, Maximian was probably put to death on Constantine's orders, even though the official version was that he had committed suicide). And now, even though Maxentius had not lived in harmony with his father, he now assumed the attitude of a loving son. Expecting a war in the north, he assembled a large host of ground troops: 170,000 foot and 18,000 horse. He brought some of these troops from the recently recovered African provinces. As a precaution, he reinforced Rome's formidable defensive walls and assembled substantial food supplies.

Constantine Marches on Rome

Dalmatius took command of Licinius's legions and concentrated them in what is now northern Serbia and Croatia.

This made it seem like the main attack on Italy would come from that direction. Expecting this, Maxentius concentrated most of his forces at the foot of the northeastern Alps and placed his supply depots and headquarters at the opposite end of the valley, in Verona. Maxentius was probably preparing a daring operation: marching up the Adige valley and forcing his way through the Alpine passes to capture Rhetia and Noricum, i.e., the lands of today's southern Germany and Austria.[62]

But Constantine pre-empted Maxentius' plans. In a lightning-fast move, he crossed the western Alps at the end of summer. He led a small force—only about thirty thousand men—but these were his best troops. For the most part, they were Germans.

The first city where he encountered the enemy was Segusio, today's Susa, in the Italian Piedmont. The city gave up without a fight. Prudently, Constantine stopped his soldiers from looting. The news of this quickly spread throughout Italy, preceding the march of the invading army and persuading the population not to resist the invader.

Now, Constantine advanced eastward. He obliterated Maximian's cavalry at Turin, and the city opened its gates. Soon after, Milan surrendered. At Brixia—today's Brescia—Constantine defeated the enemy cavalry again. Heavy fighting came only near Verona. The

---

[62] The importance of Noricum lay in the quality of its iron ore deposits. While ancient Romans did not understand the chemistry, smelting iron from Noricum deposits resulted in a carbon-rich iron, comparable in tensile strength to modern steel.

prefect of Maxentius's Praetorians tried to come to the relief of the beleaguered city but was killed in an extremely bloody battle. Verona capitulated. The remaining centers of northern Italy—Mantua and Aquileia, were taken relatively easily.

But the war was not yet over. Rome had to be captured first, and recent events had shown how difficult that could be. Several years earlier, Severus had had to retreat from beneath the mighty walls of the imperial capital and, after him, Galerius himself. Nevertheless, Constantine bravely crossed the arc of the Apennines and marched straight south.

At the Milvian Bridge

Again, Maxentius intended to defend himself within the city walls, but he changed his plans almost at the last minute and led his troops out to accept a battle in the open field.

It is difficult to say what influenced the decision. Probably both superstition and the situation in the city. October 28 was approaching, and with it, the sixth anniversary of his ascension to power. The emperor probably thought that that day, once so fortunate for him, would again bring him triumph. Likewise, the Sibylline books, which he consulted, announced: "On this day, the enemy of Rome will die." Maxentius naturally assumed that the "enemy of Rome" was Constantine.

But perhaps his most important reason was that the people of Rome had turned against him. When the emperor held circus games to celebrate his sixth anniversary, riots broke out, and the crowds chanted: Constantine Invictus! Hostile sentiments were common both among the poor and the rich.

Most government officials felt that the cause of Maxentius had been lost and that it was necessary to curry favor with the incoming ruler. It was general knowledge that Constantine's rule in Gaul was relatively mild, and now news came that his army in Italy was doing well. So, instead of enduring the hardships and dangers of a siege, it seemed better to surrender without a fight—or so many thought.

The battle which the two emperors fought on October 28, 312, bears in history the name of the Battle of the Milvian Bridge. The bridge spanned the Tiber a few kilometers north of Rome, where Via Flaminia—a road leading through Umbria to the Adriatic coast—crossed the Tiber. Just beyond the Milvian Bridge, that road connected to Via Cassia, which led to Etruria and Florence. Constantine's army descended down that road. Maxentius blocked its advance in front of the bridge.

Given the sparse and partly contradictory descriptions we find in the sources, neither the exact location of the battlefield nor the reconstruction of its course is possible. At any rate, it seems that the stone Milvian Bridge had been partially demolished on Maxentius's orders to impede Constantine's advance. He had given that order back when he was still planning to defend himself within the city walls.

Now, the stone bridge had to be hastily repaired, and a pontoon bridge set up next to it to allow Maxentius's army to cross.

When the battle came, the Praetorian cohorts fought valiantly. Years earlier, they had given power to Maxentius and owed numerous privileges to him. However, when the rest of the army began to retreat, the Praetorians also broke ranks. Meanwhile, the pontoon bridge on the Tiber broke up—it may have been the work of saboteurs. The fleeing masses of Maxentius's men trashed against each other and pushed into the current swollen with autumnal rains.

Maxentius crossed the Tiber on horseback. However, as his steed ascended the steep bank, it slipped and fell into deep water. The emperor's heavy armor weighed him down. He drowned. The victors retrieved the corpse from the river. Wishing to prove that the war was over and that Maxentius had died, Constantine ordered the head to be cut off, impaled on a spear, and carried around the city. Clouds of gawkers converged, taunting the dead emperor and spitting. Not that they particularly hated Maxentius, but it seems that any commoner relishes the opportunity to jeer fallen greats, just as he is happy to grovel before them while they are in power. Afterward, the head was sent to Africa so that the people there could also see for themselves the proof of Maxentius's defeat.

Constantine made a triumphant entry into Rome the day after the battle: October 29. The term "triumphant entry" should be understood figuratively: this was not an official triumph—the stately procession up the Via Sacra to the Capitol, which had been the privilege of victorious commanders and emperors since time immemorial. Constantine could not hold such a triumph, for he had defeated not an external enemy but an opponent in a civil war. All the same, the crowds greeted him with enthusiasm. The Senate received Constantine with honors but also with fear. The Senators were terrified that the new ruler would begin his reign like almost all of his predecessors had done: by removing former dignitaries and depriving them of their titles, estates, and frequently—their heads.

The victor, however, acted magnanimously, demonstrating great political wisdom. He deferred with ostentatious respect to the Senate as an institution symbolizing the continuity of the Roman state. In a certain sense, he even humbled himself before the venerable assembly since he accepted the title *Maximus Augustus*, that is, the Greatest Augustus—or Senior Augustus—from its hands. He thus honored the Senate as the supreme instance of legitimacy. With this title, Constantine formally became the head of the Empire and the incarnation of its symbolic unity. At the same time, Maxentius was posthumously declared an enemy of the people, and a resolution was passed stating that the name of the tyrant should be erased from all official documents and inscriptions.

The victor now completed the huge building that Maxentius had begun at the Forum Romanum to serve as a place for court hearings and public ceremonies and gave it his name—*Basilica Constantini*.

The Legend of the Symbol:
the Monogram on the Shields

Because Maxentius had treated Christians well, Constantine could not have presented himself as a defender of an oppressed religion—even if he had been a follower of it by then. It was clear to all that the war of 312 arose from pure power politics, and for the people of Italy, only two questions were relevant: which ruler would be more lenient in the matters of taxation and which would treat his subjects more humanely. Addressing these questions, Constantine's propaganda, both then and later, portrayed Maxentius as a ruthless tyrant. Nevertheless, at some later point, the legend arose that Constantine had acted in AD 312 as a defender of persecuted Christians. This legend still finds its defenders today. It proclaims that the emperor was already a professed Christian by AD 312 and was victorious because, before the Battle of the Milvian Bridge, he placed the symbol of Christ on the shields of his soldiers.

Why should this story be considered a legend? We will find the answer by tracing its origins. To do so, we will have to get a little ahead of our story.

First off, the story comes from Lactantius:

> The anniversary of Maxentius taking power—October 28, was approaching: his five-year reign was coming to an end. Constantine received an admonition in his sleep that he should place the celestial sign of God on his shields and then go into battle. He did as he was told. He inscribed Christ on his shields: the letter I bent at the top and passed through the letter X. His army, armed with this sign, took to the field.[63]

Thus, if Lactantius is to be believed, Constantine had a prophetic dream just before the decisive battle, perhaps on the night of October 27-28. He immediately ordered the Greek monogram of the name *Christos* to be painted on his army's shields. This monogram consisted

---

[63] Lactantius 44

of the letter *X* (in the Greek alphabet, that letter reads *chi*) crossed with an *I* with a bent top, that is, shaped somewhat like our "P" (which reads *rho* in Greek). We often find this symbol in the archeology of the period, especially on tombstones. It is sometimes referred to by the names of the two Greek letters that make it up: *chi-rho*:

Lactantius' account seems persuasive, as all its elements can be explained rationally. After all, we remember that Constantine's official propaganda proclaimed as early as 310 that Apollo had appeared to him. Why shouldn't a similar story be repeated now? If two years earlier, the cult of the Sun-God could have been exploited for political purposes, why might not now a Christian symbol be used in the same way in the new situation?

But upon closer examination, doubts arise. Here are some relevant facts:

1. We find no symbol that could even remotely be interpreted as Christian on Constantine's coins before AD315, while we see plenty of symbols and inscriptions related to the cult of Sol Invictus. Moreover, Constantine's mints continued to issue coins with clearly pagan themes until 320, and occasionally even later.

2. In 315, the triumphal Arch of Constantine was finally completed on the orders of the Senate. We will have a chance to discuss that structure later, but we can now point out that no decorative element of this monument refers in any detail, even the smallest and the most indirect way, to Christianity, while many speak clearly of the worship of the Sun. Suffice it to recall the sun chariot ascending to the sky. The inscription on the arch says that the emperor defeated the tyrant (that is, Maxentius) *instinctu divinitatis*, i.e., by "divine

inspiration." But what divinity inspired him? Various concepts can be put under this vague term. *Divinitas* was then in common use in Neoplatonic philosophy.

3. The same is true of a eulogy in honor of the emperor delivered in Trier in 313, in the presence of Constantine. In it, *divinitas* is mentioned several times as the ruler's guardian and advisor. In one place, the eulogy even refers to "the creator god and lord of the world." This seems to establish beyond doubt that the emperor was already inclined to monotheism, that is, to the worship of only one deity. But which? Some listeners may have thought the words referred to the Sun God; Christians probably rejoiced that the emperor was moving closer to their beliefs.

It is clear that a gradual evolution had been taking place in Constantine's religious politics since 310: through the worship of the Sun-God towards philosophical monotheism, which, although in different variations, was the prevailing stance among the intellectuals of the time. A very beautiful—and interesting—example of this are the words in the last part of the eulogy: they sound like a solemn prayer:

> Thee we implore and beseech, O Supreme Creator of all things, who have as many names as you have willed to establish languages; for we cannot know what you yourself desire to be called; whether you are some force or thought divine, which, pours out all over the world and, merging with each of the elements, without any impulse from without, sets them in motion all by itself; or are you a power residing above the highest heavens, looking down upon your animate creation from the highest castle of nature.
>
> Thee, I say, we implore and beseech: deign to preserve this ruler for us for all eternity![64]

These kinds of vague formulations were easily reconciled with any cult and any system of thought; they could satisfy both the subtle intellectual and the simplest of men. Thus, when the orator delivered this confession of faith in the magnificent hall of Trier's palace, he knew that he would find the understanding of many and, most

---

[64] *Panegyric* IX 2, 4, 5, 16, 26

importantly, that of the ruler himself.

Gradually, however, this philosophical monotheism of Constantine began to take on an increasingly distinct Christian hue. Many factors contributed to this and purely political considerations played a significant role. The transformations were relatively slow and cautious. The emperor initially avoided all explicitness, using symbolic imagery and statements that lent themselves to various interpretations. One thing is clear: in light of the available documents, there can be no question of any sudden conversion or religious breakthrough in Constantine's life.

The Legend of the Symbol: the Six-pointed Star

Does it follow that Lactantius—or perhaps his informants—simply made up the symbol on the shields? That would be the easy explanation, but the matter is complex. First of all, we should keep in mind that Lactantius wrote his work at the court of Crispus, son of Constantine, probably between 318 and 320. An explicitly pro-Christian orientation had triumphed in the emperor's entourage by then. But there hung in the air a growing conflict between Constantine and Licinius, the ruler of the eastern part of the Empire. As early as 313, while fighting Maximianus Daza, Licinius demonstrated his favor and preferment for the new religion. On the night before the decisive battle between the two—a matter we will present in more detail later—he is said to have had a vision: an angel revealed to him in what words he and his army should pray in order to win. In that case, the story made sense: there were many Christians in Daza's army. The idea was, therefore, to win them over. The idea proved successful, and Licinius crushed his opponent.

Constantine learned his lesson. When relations between him and Licinius became strained, he showed as much favor to the Christians as possible. So if, as it was said, Licinius had defeated Daza thanks to a divinely revealed prayer, Constantine could not be far behind: his triumph over Maxentius must also have been the work of heaven. Constantine's advisors recalled that his soldiers at the battle at the Milvian Bridge had the sign of a six-pointed star-burst on their shields, that is, an X crossed with a vertical dash:

Admittedly, this sign has been used for centuries, in various countries and in many variations, usually as a solar or astral symbol. It was also used by Christians because it was the monogram of their Lord (in the Greek alphabet: *Khristos Iesus*) and, at the same time, his symbol as the Sun of Justice. It is quite understandable that Constantine, a follower of the Unconquered Sun, even wishing to pass himself off as its incarnation, used this sign on the shields of his armies, and perhaps no one at the time thought it could be understood in any other way. Later, however, in the new situation, it was easy to claim that it had been a Christian symbol all along.

We have already mentioned that this sign first appeared on Constantine's coins in 315 as an emblem on the imperial helmet, but even there, it could have meant the Invincible Sun. It does not appear as a distinctly Christian symbol until after 324, that is, after Constantine's victory over Licinius.[65]

---

⁶⁵ *Sylloge Inscriptionum Christianum Veterum Museia Vaticani*, Helsinki-Helsingfors 1965, II 156-160 (ed. By P. Bruun).

The Legend of the Symbol: the Statue of Constantine

Soon after his victory at the Milvian Bridge, the Senate, wishing to honor Constantine, passed a resolution to erect a statue of him. It seems that it was set up in the Forum Romanum, perhaps inside the Basilica of Maxentius. Who knows if it wasn't the same giant statue, fragments of which are displayed today at the Capitoline Museum: the emperor's magnificent head is particularly impressive.

Eusebius, who never visited Rome, wrote about this statue in his *History of the Church* this way:

> Constantine immediately ordered that the victorious Symbol (*tropaion*) of Salvation be placed in the hand of this statue. This statue, holding the Sign of Salvation, was exhibited in the most frequented place in Rome. Then, he ordered that the following Latin inscription be placed on it:

> "In this sign, which is the proof of my virtue, I saved you and liberated your city from the yoke of the tyrant, restoring you to your former freedom."[66]

But earlier in his account, while speaking of the war with Maxentius, Eusebius does not say one word about either the alleged vision of Constantine or that the shields of his troops were adorned with any special symbol. Instead, he limits himself to a very brief and general assertion:

> Constantine took pity on those in Rome who were groaning under the rule of the tyrant. He invoked in prayer the heavenly God and his Word, the Savior of all, Jesus Christ, as his ally. Then, he set out with his entire army, pledging to the Romans that he would restore to them the freedom they had enjoyed in the days of their forefathers.[67]

---

[66] Eusebius IX 9, 10-11
[67] Eusebius IX 9, 2

It is hard to imagine that Eusebius, who in his later years came into personal contact with the emperor, would have completely omitted the matter of the vision and the sign on the shields if either were a historical fact—or even the current tale.

And here is a seemingly paradoxical thing: it is precisely Eusebius's account of the "sign of salvation" in the hand of Constantine's statue that indirectly reinforces the view, advanced in the previous chapter, that the shields of the emperor's army bore the sign of a six-pointed star. For it is simply inconceivable that a statue of a ruler with a cross in his hand would have been placed in the heart of the city of Rome at that time. We should remember that the Senate was then in its vast majority pagan and attached to ancient traditions; it remained so for a long time afterward; and Christianity was not a significant political force on the Tiber. In such a situation, and in a city that had only just been conquered, an official and overt manifestation of a foreign minority religion would have been downright irresponsible—even if he had indeed become a Christian by then. Indeed, over the next several years, Constantine avoided all symbols of the new faith, even on coins.

On the other hand, it is highly probable that a statue of Constantine in Rome had some religious sign, and perhaps it was the same sign of the six-pointed star. Some scholars make another suggestion: that the statue held a military banner—the *vexillum*—which was basically shaped like a cross: a long staff with a crossbar from which hung a vertical banner:

Those who so wished may have seen a Christian symbol in either sign.[68]

In either case, some indirect evidence suggests that the statue was pagan in nature. In 313, a eulogy was delivered in Trier before the emperor. It clearly stated that the statue erected in Rome by the Senate depicted the ruler as a god.[69] If so, Constantine undoubtedly resembled Apollo since, in the year 310, the deity appeared to him, taking on his form and facial features. And if the statue held a religious symbol, then it probably held some sort of a solar emblem.

The Legend of the Symbol: the Phenomenon in the Sky

The legend of the symbol assumed its final shape only after Constantine's death. It did so mainly thanks to a hagiographic work entitled *The Life of Constantine*. Its author was allegedly our Eusebius of Caesarea. The story is clearly fictionalized, although the writer insists that he heard it from the mouth of the emperor himself, who supposedly confirmed the truth of his words by... an oath. Here is the account:

> While still in Gaul and preparing his expedition against Maxentius, the emperor begged this god, whom his father served, to reveal Himself to him and help him in the coming war. And while in prayer, he saw an unusual phenomenon in the sky, which the entire army also saw along with him. It was early afternoon; a luminous cross shone above the sun, and on it was the inscription: "In this sign you shall win."

The account does not say in what language these words appeared; since the account is written in Greek, it also quotes them in Greek.

---

[68] C. Ch. Picard, *Les Trophees Romains*, Paris 1957, p. 504-506
[69] Panegyric IX 25

> Now, upon seeing this omen, everyone was amazed and horrified.
> The emperor pondered until nightfall how he should understand
> the strange symbol. Then, in a dream, he saw Christ carrying the
> same symbol that had just appeared in the sky. The Lord
> commanded the emperor to make an exact likeness of the sign and
> use it to fight his enemies. The very next day, Constantine told his
> friends about his vision. He summoned goldsmiths, sat among
> them, described the appearance of the sign in detail, and ordered
> them to make it out of gold and precious stones.

To lend credence to his argument, the author adds: "By the grace of
the emperor, I too was able to see this symbol with my own eyes," and
he includes a description of it:

> The tall, gold-covered shaft had a wreath of gold and precious stones
> at the top, inside of which were the initials of Christ: the letter *rho*
> (P) intersected the letter *khi* (X). Below, on the crosspiece, was fixed
> a square piece of precious cloth woven with gold and jewels, while
> below, on the shaft itself, were the likenesses of Constantine and his
> sons.
>
> After making this sign, the emperor summoned Christian priests.
> These explained to him who the Deity that appeared to him was and
> the meaning of the cross. From then on, the emperor decided to
> worship only this Deity and remain faithful to Him.[70]

So much for *The Life of Constantine*. A few words are enough to show
how blatantly unreliable this story is.

The symbol so accurately depicted is, in fact, an imperial
banner. It served the Roman armies not only then but even in the
Byzantine period, and in a sense, it lives on to this day, albeit in a highly
simplified form, as an ecclesiastical ensign. Iconographic sources give
different variations of it, but the basic form remained the same for
many centuries. This kind of banner was called *labarum*. It first
appeared around the year 325, at a time when Constantine had already
firmly committed himself to Christianity and, having previously
fought against Licinius, ostentatiously used the symbolism of the new

---

[70] *The Life of Constantine*, I 27-31

religion. In short, the author of *The Life of Constantine*, probably writing in the second half of the fourth century, wants to surround the *labarum* with a nimbus of divinity: it is supposed to be a banner revealed by Christ Himself. In fact, the *labarum* should be regarded as a natural development of the old Roman battle emblems.

The fictitiousness of the story is clearly proven by one fact: Constantine had long lived in the East, where he certainly had had the opportunity to get acquainted with the beliefs and symbols of Christians.[71]

The Cursed Plague of Informers

Constantine stayed in Rome for less than three months: he entered the city at the end of October 312 and left soon after January 20 of the following year. However, he accomplished quite a lot in this short period, and his legislative acts passed while in the capital perfectly characterize Constantine as a man and a ruler.

As is usual with every change of government, in the autumn of 312, there appeared in Rome a multitude of individuals who thought they had been handed down a great opportunity to settle old scores and give vent to envy while at the same time gaining favor with the new emperor and attaining either wealth or a lucrative position, or both. There was a sudden flood of denunciations against all those who had held important positions under Maxentius. But the informers— they were called *delatores*—met with an unpleasant surprise. Constantine treated the senators and dignitaries very kindly and punished only a few of Maxentius's partisans. On the other hand, as early as December 1, an imperial edict was posted in the Forum of Trajan, proclaiming:

We must destroy one of the greatest evils of mankind, the accursed

---

[71] For a thorough discussion see J. Moreau, *Sur la vision de Constantin, Revue des Etudes Anbciennes*, LV 1953, 307-333

plague of informers. At the first opportunity, they must be seized by the throat, and the tongue of envy must be torn out with its root. Judges must not hear the accusations. Whenever any such person appears, he should suffer the death penalty.[72]

The vehemence with which the emperor denounces this scourge of the world is downright astonishing. In the mechanism of imperial bureaucratic rule, informers—though hated and despised—played a huge role that was both strictly defined and difficult to replace. We should remember that the Roman judiciary did not know the institution of the public prosecutor. Yet, this emperor believed that certain social values were far more deserving than consolidating power through fear.

Among Constantine's other decisions of the period, his attitude to the Senate and to the Praetorians are notable. In a proclamation to the Senate dated January 13, 313, the ruler resolved:

> The matter of the persons whom the tyrant [Maxentius] has removed from your midst I leave up to your judgment. Choose from among them the people who are suitable by property status, noble birth, and character. The Prefect of Rome will give us their names so that we may approve your decision.[73]

But Constantine showed no mercy for the Praetorians, the mainstay of Maxentius's rule. Their cohorts were disbanded, and their camp liquidated. This was the end of a formation that had often played a decisive role in the Empire over the previous three centuries, elevating and deposing emperors. The veterans of the units were dispersed and incorporated into frontier garrisons.

Finally, at the very end of the emperor's stay in Rome, on January 20, an edict on taxation was issued. It attempted to defend the poor against abuses by tax officials, for these, in collusion with the rich, "burdened the less wealthy beyond measure."[74] The emperor wished to be seen as a defender of the people of the lower estate, the *inferiores*,

---

[72] C. Th. X 10,2

[73] C. Th. XIV 4, 2

[74] C. Th. XIII 10, 1

against the mighty, the *potentiores*. This was to remain a key plank of his political program in the future.

Part Three
FROM MILAN TO NICAEA

The Council of Milan

The news from Italy was very painful for Maximinus Daza to hear. He lost an ally. Licinius was now free to concentrate all his forces in the East and try to seize Asia Minor. In the new situation, Daza felt that he had to pretend that he accepted the changes. He acknowledged the Senate's resolution, which granted Constantine the title of First Augustus, though this honor should have gone to him by the rules of seniority. If he manifested dissatisfaction, it was only in the form of acidic allusions to Constantine. He also embraced Galerius's Edict of Toleration. He stopped all persecution and restored total freedom to profess Christianity. (Admittedly, he was reminded of the edict by Constantine and Licinius in a pointed joint letter).

In February 313, Constantine arrived in Milan. As did Licinius. The official reason for their meeting was the marriage of Licinius to Constance, now his fiancée of almost three years. But, the two rulers took the opportunity to review the situation and agree on certain policies. The problem of Christianity was also discussed, but no new decisions were made. No joint decree was issued. The so-called "Edict of Milan," so famous in history, was never actually issued. We will see later how this term appeared in scholarship.

The reunion of the emperors was commemorated by the mints of both rulers with coins with appropriate inscriptions and images. Particularly beautiful and interesting is the gold medal, issued in Spanish Tarracona. It depicts the bust of Constantine, seen in profile, against the background of the same bust of the Sun God. The deity in question is easily recognized by its radiant crown—his permanent attribute. Constantine holds a shield, which is decorated with a very characteristic relief: the Sun rises upward on a chariot drawn by four horses; the god extends his right hand in a gesture of blessing; behind him are a star and the sickle of the moon; under the hooves of the steeds sit, on one side, the god Oceanus, emerging from the waves of the sea, on the other, the goddess of the Earth. As a whole, the symbolism of the medal is very clear, especially when we note that the Sun's profile is strikingly similar to that of Constantine. So, the emperor, being the incarnation of the universal deity, is expected to rule over the entire circumference of the earth, over all lands and seas, just like the sun. Indeed, Constantine has the facial features of the divine Sun on many of his coins: the official story of the vision in Apollo's temple in Gaul, when the god appeared to Constantine under the guise of the emperor's own features, was still taken seriously. How can one reconcile the symbolism of the Tarraconian medal, which is by no means unique, with the claim that Constantine underwent a religious conversion in 312 and became a Christian?

From Milan, Constantine went to Gaul. At the end of May, we find him in Trier, where a certain edict is dated. Licinius, on the other hand, hurried east because alarming news had arrived: Maximinus Daza had begun hostilities. He had crossed the Bosphorus and was besieging Byzantium.

The Battle of the Ergenus Field

It is hardly surprising that Daza decided to take advantage of what he thought was a great opportunity—Licinius's trip to Italy. He was in Syria, and winter was coming, but despite the distance and the inauspicious season, he moved quickly and, in a series of forced marches, crossed Asia Minor. The road led through mountains and high plateaus, and the cold, snow, freezing rain, and mud were hard on his people and animals. However, Daza did not heed the hardships and did not care about the losses. He understood that surprise gave him the best chance of victory. And he led a considerable force. When he crossed the Bosphorus and stood at the walls of Byzantium, his army still numbered about seventy thousand.

Licinius's garrison in Byzantium was small, and it surrendered after just eleven days. Maximinus then occupied Perinthos, a city on the coast of the Propontis, and only then advanced inland. He stopped after just eighteen miles, for he had a report that Licinius was already in Adrianopol, eighteen miles away. (Adrianopol is today's Edirne, on the Bulgarian-Turkish border).

Licinius had not managed to assemble all his troops but decided to block the invader's route at Adrianople anyway. He was probably planning to give battle only after the arrival of the Danube legions, but it happened otherwise. Here is Lactantius:

> An angel of God stood by the sleeping Licinius and admonished him to rise quickly and pray with the entire army to the Supreme God, saying that if he did, he would win. It seemed to Licinius that he was awake and that this angel was standing beside him, instructing him in what manner and with what words to pray. When at last he actually woke up, he summoned his secretary and dictated the prayer to him as he heard them:
>
> "Oh, you, the most High God, Thee we beseech, Thee Holy God, Thee we beseech! To Thee, we entrust our just cause, to Thee, we entrust our salvation, to Thee, we entrust our Empire. To Thee, we entrust life, victory, and happiness. Supreme, Holy God, hear our prayer. We reach our hands to Thee. Hear us, O Holy, Supreme God!"
>
> The words were transcribed in many copies and distributed among the officers so that everyone could learn the prayer by heart. Thus, everyone was inspired, believing profoundly that their victory had been preordained by heaven.

Licinius decided to fight on May 1. It was the eighth anniversary of the elevation of Maximinus Daza to the dignity of Caesar, and he set up his army on the morning of April 30, believing that the following day, his anniversary, would bring him victory. In Licinius' camp, shouts immediately arose that the enemy was moving into battle. The soldiers grabbed their weapons and moved to attack. Between the two armies stretched a large empty meadow called Campus Ergenus so the troops could see each other perfectly as they approached. At one point, Licinius' men laid down their shields, took off their helmets, stretched out their hands to the sky, and, following the example of their officers and the emperor, pronounced the words of the prayer. The enemy army heard them well while they repeated the prayer three times. Then, full of courage, Licinius's men donned their helmets and raised their shields.

The two rulers walked out in front of their formations to hold talks. However, it proved impossible to persuade Daza to make peace. He despised Licinius and hoped to get his men to come over to him; for everyone knew that Licinius was not very generous with his men, while Daza paid his army well. He had started the war with the belief that he would be able to take over Licinius' army without a fight. He then planned to attack Constantine at the head of both armies.

The ranks were already close together. Trumpets sounded, and the battle insignia went up. The Licinians were the first to attack. Their opponents, on the other hand, suddenly seized with fear, managed neither to take out their swords nor even to throw away their shields. Daza ran about the battlefield, trying to sow confusion among his opponents with promises of great gifts.

However, no one listened to him. And when an attack was launched in his direction, he cowardly turned back towards the rear.

When Daza finally realized how bad his affairs were going, he threw off the purple and fled in the rags of a slave. Half of his army fell on the battlefield, while the rest surrendered or scattered.

Daza crossed the Bosphorus Strait on May 1, that is, within a day. The next night, he was already in Nicomedia, which is one hundred and sixty miles from the battlefield. From there, he took his children, wife, and a handful of comrades and hurried east. He stopped only in Cappadocia, in eastern Asia Minor. There, he gathered soldiers around him and brought reinforcements from neighboring provinces. There, he also put the purple back on.[75]

Licinius and Christians

What was the real reason for Licinius's splendid and unexpected victory? The cited facts provide a sufficient answer by themselves: Licinius crushed Daza because he was able to pull numerous Christians to his side. Daza's rule in the East had long ago alienated the followers of the new religion, and they were very numerous there. Thus, now that Licinius had clearly and loudly sided with them at the decisive moment, they saw no reason to defend the emperor who had persecuted their religion. Many soldiers refused to take part in the battle, and many also left the ranks. Even his bodyguard abandoned Daza—about which Lactantius is strangely silent. There was no miracle. Instead, there was a simple betrayal.

Propaganda spread by Licinius's entourage sought to portray him as a fighter for God's cause. Very ancient literary tropes were used for the purpose, such as a divine messenger appearing to the commander in his sleep. (Just such a scene can be found in the oldest work of Greek literature, the *Iliad*: King Agamemnon, in his camp at Troy, sees a messenger from Zeus at his bedside, who calls on him to lead the troops into the field the following day).

No explicitly Christian term appears in the battlefield prayer of Liciunius, but Christians may well have understood it to be addressed to their God. It is difficult to say whether the text of the prayer was really transcribed and distributed among the soldiers before the battle. On the other hand, it is virtually certain that this was reported—and soon after the battle, too. Lactantius, residing then in nearby Nicomedia, heard the story from the soldiers of Licinius as they

---

[75] Lactantius 46-47

entered the city in pursuit of Maximinus.

Licinius remained in Nicomedia for an entire month. On June 13, a copy of a letter written by the emperor to the governor of the local province, Bithynia, appeared on the walls of the city. This document, one of the most famous in the history of our cultural milieu, is known to us both in its Latin version, transmitted by Lactantius, and in its Greek translation, preserved in Eusebius.

The So-Called Edict of Milan

When we happily came together in Milan, Emperor Constantine and I, and discussed matters of public welfare and security, we deemed it necessary to issue, among other decrees which, in our opinion, would benefit our people, also one which relates to the worship of the gods, namely, that both Christians and all others should be given complete freedom to profess whatever religion they wished. In this way, it will be possible to placate all the heavenly gods and dispose of them favorably towards us and all our subjects.

Therefore, guided by such sound and proper reasoning, we have deemed it necessary to make this determination: we believe that no one should be hindered whether he gives his soul to the Christian faith or to any other religion which he himself judges most suitable for himself; and this so that the Supreme Deity, whom we all worship, each according to his own convictions, may in all circumstances shower us with its usual favor and kindness.

Therefore, may it be known to Your Eminence that all the restrictions on Christians that have been ordered in previous letters sent to Your Office are now removed, and whosoever now wishes to profess the Christian faith may continue to do so openly and freely without being subjected to any investigation or other annoyances. We thought it necessary to state this as clearly as possible so that you may know that we have given these Christians complete and absolute freedom to profess their religion. And since we have granted this permission to them, may Your Eminence understand that in the interest of peace in our time, we have also left to others the unlimited and complete freedom to choose their religion or creed so that everyone may freely worship whatever deity he chooses. For we do not wish to do any religion any disservice on our part.

The letter continues with orders that all buildings and property confiscated from Christian communities should be returned to them free of charge; and that whoever had purchased Christian property or received it as a gift and now stood, as a result, to lose it could apply to the local governor for compensation. The letter ends with an exhortation:

And in order that word of this our will and benevolence may reach the general public, it is necessary to post it everywhere, to announce it and make it known to the general public, so that this legislative action of our benevolence may be known to all.[76]

This order is traditionally referred to as the "Edict of Milan," and Constantine is often said to be its author. However, these claims seem unfounded. In legal terms, this is not an edict but an imperial circular. The author of the letter is certainly Licinius himself; he is acting in the spirit of the Conference of Milan, during which the two rulers came to the conclusion that the Edict of Tolerance issued by Galerius in 311 should be implemented. However, in Licinius' letter, we find a novelty: a promise to return confiscated church property and to pay compensation to those who would now have to renounce it. The question arises who the originator of this provision was. Perhaps the idea came from Constantine since it would have been far easier for him to implement it: in the western provinces, persecutions had been light and short-lived, so the issue of possible compensation was not a major economic problem. Things were different in the East. But Constantine may have been either unaware of this or deliberately wished to cause difficulties for the two rulers of the East—Licinius and Maximinus Daza.

---

[76] Lactantius 48

In the heading of the letter, Licinius also lists Constantine as its co-author and even places his name above his own. This is entirely consistent with the chancellery practice of the time. For although the empire had several rulers, it remained formally a unity, and thanks to a resolution of the Senate, Constantine was entitled to the title of its Elder, or First Augustus.

No equivalent letter of Constantine has survived. What we do have, however, are several letters and decrees indicating that he also acted with great zeal in the same spirit.

However, before we discuss those documents, we should outline the fate of the defeated Maximinus Daza.

The Death of Maximinus Daza

His disastrous defeat forced Daza to change his religious policy. As soon as news of Licinius's decrees reached him, he immediately followed suit. In June or July of 313, an Edict of Maximunus Daza appeared, granting Christians all freedoms. In its preamble, the emperor stated that he had already put tolerant policies into practice but that officials had exceeded their authority and distorted the intent of his decrees. He now decreed:

> People who wish to belong to this religion are now allowed, by virtue of our grace, to practice it as they choose for themselves, as they desire, and as they like. It is also permitted to build any manner of houses of worship. And out of a surfeit of benevolence, we have deemed it good to issue the following decree:

> Any house or piece of land formerly owned by a Christian and forfeited to the state treasury on the orders of our Fathers [that is, Diocletian and Galerius] must now be returned to the said Christian, regardless of whether it was then further sold on or donated. For in this regard, all should feel our devotion and care.[77]

---

[77] Eusebius IX 10

All the same, the days of Maximinus Daza were numbered. The victorious armies of Licinius were approaching eastern Asia Minor. The ruler of the East still tried to organize resistance but fell seriously ill. Eventually, it seems, he committed suicide. This happened in the Cilician city of Tarsus at the end of August or the beginning of September 313.

Both Lactantius and Eusebius draw a picture of the suffering of the "tyrant" in his last days with an almost sadistic relish. According to Eusebius, he died digested by fever and starvation, emaciated, skeleton-like, rolling on the ground in terrible pain. Lactantius maintains that the unbearable suffering drove him mad; for four days, he ate only earth. He attempted suicide by beating his head against a wall. Both writers agree that by the end of his illness, he had gone completely blind; his eyes are said to have fallen out of their orbits.

If Eusebius is to be believed, the victor dealt with the high officials of Maximinus Daza very harshly. They all suffered death, most after terrible tortures. An equally harsh fate befell members of the imperial family, regardless of age or gender. Daza's eight-year-old son and seven-year-old daughter were killed, while his wife was drowned in the Orontes. Also killed were all those who had previously sought refuge at his court. Particularly pathetic was the end of Diocletian's wife, Prisca, and his daughter, Galerius' widow, Valeria. Both went into hiding for months, disguised as simple women. Captured after a year and a half in Greece, in Thessalonica, they were stabbed to death and their bodies thrown into the sea.

Diocletian was probably dead by then. Accounts of his death are contradictory, so it is difficult to determine its exact cause and time. Some believe that the creator of the tetrarchy departed this world only in 316. But one thing is absolutely certain: the old man saw the total collapse of his work.

Constantine to Anullinus and Ceacilianus

Probably just after the Milan meeting, perhaps as early as March 313, Constantine sent an official letter to Anullinus, proconsul of Africa. In it, he recommended that private individuals return to Christian communities all confiscated property. He motivated this order in very vague terms:

> Our love of goodness always preserves this custom so that what is someone else's property not only does not suffer any damage but even returns to its former ownership.[78]

Note: there is no mention in the letter of any possible compensation for the individuals who will now have to surrender the formerly Christian property, however legally they acquired it. In this regard, Constantine proved more "frugal" than Licinius, who in his letter provided for the possibility of indemnification, although, as far as we can see, he never issued an executive order on the matter.

At the same time, Constantine wrote to the most prominent ecclesiastical dignitary in Africa, Caecilianus, bishop of Carthage. He informed him that he was granting an allowance "to the ministers of the legal and most enlightened Catholic church for their expenses;" Ursus, the head of the finances of the African diocese, had already received an order to transfer to Caecilianus the sum of three thousand *folles*, which in turn Caecilianus should now distribute among the priests, but only according to a list, sent to him by Hosius. And, in the event that this sum proved insufficient, Caecilianus was supposed to demand additional amounts from the administrator of the imperial estates in Africa.[79]

Hosius is mentioned here without any further explanation as a person well-known to the addressee. Indeed, he was a highly respected figure in the Christian world. Around the year 296, he assumed the dignity of the bishop of Corduba, present-day Cordoba

---

[78] Ibid., X 5

[79] Ibid., X 6

in Spain; he suffered persecution during the reign of Maximian and took part in the synod of Spanish bishops in the city of Elvira in 306. We do not know where and when Constantine first encountered him; it may have happened as early as 311 when he seized Spain. In any case, the bishop managed to win the ruler's trust very quickly. He went on to exert an enormous influence on the formation of his religious views, although, as we shall see, Constantine was to pursue a very cautious policy in this area for many years to come. Hosius became his advisor on matters of Christianity and, for this reason, was entrusted with many important and sensitive missions. This is our first preserved document to mention him as a member of the imperial entourage.

But why is it that the roster of priests who are to receive the allowance is prepared by Hosius in Italy, at the imperial court, rather than in Africa? Could it be that Constantine did not trust the bishop of Carthage? And why this special concern for the affairs of African Christians? At the end of the letter to Caecilianus, we find a clue as to where we should look for our answer. We read:

> It has been reported to me that certain persons of unstable mind wish to deceive the faithful of the most excellent Catholic Church by means of some false doctrine. Learn, therefore, that I have personally ordered the proconsul Anullinus and Patricius, the deputy prefect, to take due care of these matters and not neglect a problem of such importance. Therefore, if you find that any people of this kind remain in their madness, immediately turn to the aforementioned officials and submit the matter to them so they can dissuade such persons from their error, as I have instructed them to do.

It is clear from these words that there was no consensus among Christians in the African provinces. Some group fiercely fought against Caecilianus and the communities faithful to him, which was why Constantine so insistently referred to Caecilianus's followers as "the legitimate and most enlightened Catholic Church." The emperor was clearly anxious that religious disputes should not lead to political repercussions and that was why he was willing to grant Caecilianus all kinds of assistance: both financial and administrative. The list of people to whom the allowance was to be paid was prepared not in Carthage but at the imperial court simply for this reason: in order to protect Caecilianus from the accusation that he was distributing money to his supporters on his own decision.

What were the disturbances in the African church?

The Origins of the African Schism

During the years of persecution under Diocletian and Maximian, many clergy in Africa, like in many other provinces, broke down and succumbed to the demands of the authorities. The more cowardly surrendered their liturgical books to the officials; even some bishops did so. Others tried to deceive both the law and their own conscience by hiding the sacred books and giving up other, unimportant books. However, there was also a sizable group who remained steadfast and prepared to bear all consequences, including death. Persecution in Africa was brief and ended as early as the spring of 305. The steadfast triumphed and, as is perhaps only human, considered all others, regardless of their degree of guilt, as traitors and apostates—*traditores*. And they maintained that sacraments were only valid if the priest administering them had been in a state of grace at the time and that, therefore, the sin of a priest-apostate weighed upon his entire flock. And since all those who submitted during the persecution had thereby sinned mortally, the *traditores*-priests risked bringing down the divine wrath on the entire Christian Church.

This schism came to a fever pitch in 312, when Caecilianus became bishop of Carthage. He was personally blameless but was frowned upon by fanatics, for he acted with moderation toward dissenters and former apostates. Caecilianus also offended a certain very influential and wealthy lady, Lucilla, by rebuking her for the superstitious devotion she showed to the relics of martyrs. Caecilianus's enemies, unable to attack him personally, claimed that one of the bishops who had consecrated him had apostatized and, therefore, his consecration was invalid. A synod of seventy bishops deposed Caecilianus and elected Majorinus as bishop of Carthage. It was widely reported that the latter owed his election to Lucilla's gold. Caecilianus did not give up the office and, for his part, gathered many of the clergy and faithful around him. From then on, disputes and clashes took on an increasingly fierce character.

News of this conflict quickly reached Rome and caused a great deal of anxiety since the emperor was just consolidating his new acquisitions, and the African provinces were crucial because they supplied much of Rome's grain and oil. It was all the more important because Africa had strong separatist tendencies. The emperor felt, therefore, that immediate action was necessary to bring about peace and order as soon as possible.

Constantine, as we know from the letter quoted above, sided with Caecilianus. Why? Why didn't he summon representatives of both factions before him? Why did he dismiss Majorinus's supporters as troublemakers out of hand?

It seems—and this was a common opinion at the time—that Hosius played the decisive role in that decision. Hosius believed that any legitimately elected church dignitary had to be defended against radicals and extremists. (There are some indications that Hosius himself had been attacked by similar fanatics in Spain). Whatever the case, the emperor concluded that the matter would be most easily handled by giving Caecilianus financial and, if necessary, administrative support. Constantine even promised—in yet another letter to Anullius—to exempt the clergy of the African provinces who remained loyal to Caecilianus from any tax or labor obligation to the state. This second letter is also significant because in it, the emperor speaks with great reverence about Christianity, concluding with the words:

> If they [the clergy] serve God with greatest possible zeal, there will flow from it, in my opinion, a great benefit for the state.[80]

---

[80] Eusebius X 6a

However, these moves did not—and could not—bring the expected result. Rome did not appreciate the real causes of the schism in Africa. Rome thought it was just a matter of personal disputes or differences of opinion on purely religious matters. In reality, however, this conflict had its roots in the fundamental social and ethnic conflicts that had long troubled the people of Roman Africa. The supporters of Majorinus and his successors came primarily from the lower, poorer classes and from less Romanized areas, whose population, mostly Berber, resented Roman rule. African "Catholics," on the other hand, were mainly associated with the Latin-speaking landowning classes and with the Roman apparatus of power. Of course, in practice, the division was not so simple and clear; and one found people of different backgrounds on either side, but the fundamental sources of the conflict were ethnic and socio-economic, and they fueled the schism for a long time indeed—for generations and centuries—until the invasion of the Arabs in the seventh century.[81]

Donatus

On April 15, Anullinus sent a letter to the emperor, notifying him with due reverence that he had called on the African clergy to get along in concord and unity and announced that priests loyal to Caecilianus were exempt from burdens on the state. "However—writes the governor further—

> after a few days, certain persons appeared before me, accompanied by crowds of people. These individuals attacked Caecilianus and handed me two letters: one sealed, the other open. They also insisted very strongly that I forward these letters directly to the Sacred and Venerable Court of Your Divinity.

---

[81] For Donatism, see W. H. Frend, The Donatist Church, Oxforf 1952; on the social tensions in Africa, see T. Kotula, *U źródeł afrykańskiego separatyzmu w III w. naszej ery*, Wrocław, 1962

The sealed letter was titled *Accusations against Caecilianus, delivered by Majorinus and his party;* while the other, open, was a short petition:

> Most illustrious Emperor Constantine! We address you because you come from a righteous family. We also know that your Father did not persecute the Church, differing in this from other emperors. Gaul is thus free from the stain of this crime. Since there has been a dispute between us and certain other African bishops, we ask that you appoint judges from Gaul to decide the quarrel between us.[82]

The letter is our indirect but important evidence that no one knew anything about Constantine's alleged conversion to Christianity at the time. The petitioners turned to the emperor because his father had treated Christians tolerantly. However, the petition had another, almost epoch-making significance: it was probably the first formulation of the idea that a meeting of bishops convened by the emperor should be regarded as the supreme authority within the church. For the first time in history, Christians were turning to secular authority to help settle their internal affairs. Yes, a somewhat similar incident happened almost forty years earlier when Emperor Aurelian asked Western bishops to settle a dispute within the Antiochian community, but the overall situation, the gravity of the case, and the position of the Church were all very different then.

Note: the supporters of Caecilianus did not protest against this proposal, meaning that Constantine had no reason to dismiss the petition. He was probably relieved that a solution to the conflict had been proposed. He promptly sent a letter to Miltiades, the bishop of Rome:

> I have received several important letters from Anullinus, the excellent proconsul of Africa. They show that Caecilianus, bishop of Carthage, is accused of some crimes by some of his African co-religionists. It hurts me very deeply that in those very provinces which the Divine Providence has entrusted to my care of its own accord, and where there is such a multitude of inhabitants, the

---

[82] Quoted in St. Augistine, *Epistulae,* 88 and 93

people persist in mischief, dividing into different camps, and there are disagreements even among the bishops. It occurred to me, therefore, that Caecilianus, ten bishops who accuse him, and ten others who defend him, should come to Rome. They will be heard in your presence and in the presence of Rheticus [bishop of Augustodunum, today's Autun], Maternus [bishop of Cologne], and Marinus [bishop of Arelate], your colleagues, whom I have ordered to come to Rome in haste for this purpose. And, to inform you of all this as accurately as possible, I enclose copies of the letters that Anullinus has sent me, and I am also sending such copies to your aforementioned colleagues. After reading them, Your Eternity will judge for yourself how these matters should be investigated and resolved. It has probably not escaped your attention with what respect I treat the legally existing Catholic Church. Therefore, I do not want you to allow any schism or split within the church to persist anywhere.

May, O Most Honorable, the Deity of the Great God keep you in His Protection for many years to come.[83]

The letter is very polite, but in its general tone, it is not different from letters addressed by the emperor to governors and other high officials. The bishop of Rome is instructed to deal with the conflict within the African church, and at the same time, there is a clear indication which side of the conflict the emperor thinks is right. It is also worth noting the closing words: the undefined Deity of the Great God, which could be the Christian God just as easily as Apollo, the Sol Invictus.

Meanwhile, a new development took place in Africa: Majorinus died, and in his place, a new man was elected bishop: Donatus, a man who had already played a significant role in attacking Caecilianus. Donatus was a man of uncommon abilities. An excellent organizer and a great orator, he was to remain at the head of his movement in Carthage for more than forty years. Out of the chaos of small groupings, he created a compact and disciplined organization that lasted for centuries as a separate church. Rightly is the African schism known in history under the name of "Donatism."

---

[83] Eusebius X 5

The Lateran and Arelate

Miltiades greatly expanded the composition of the college of arbitrators suggested to him by the emperor, appointing to it eighteen more bishops from various cities in Italy. With such a large membership, the commission began its work on September 30, 313. Sessions were held in Rome, in a palace that had once belonged to the Laternus family of the Senatorial class but was now owned by Constantine's wife, Fausta. The verdict came at the third session on October 2. Caecilianus emerged as victor, while Donatus was reprimanded for sowing confusion, causing schism, and requiring those clerics who had apostatized during the persecution to resubmit to baptism. On the other hand, bishops ordained by Caecilianus's opponents were recognized and allowed to hold their offices.

The Donatists in Africa did not accept the verdict (Donatus himself, it seems, was detained in Italy) and soon asked Emperor Constantine to reopen the case. They argued that the Lateran commission had not sufficiently investigated all the accusations against Bishop Felix of Aptunga,[84] who had consecrated Caecilianus but had stained himself, in their view, with the mortal sin of giving up the Holy Scriptures.

Constantine accepted these appeals very reluctantly. He was reportedly disgusted by the fact that the Christian priests were arguing among themselves and litigating like pagans. But, since he did not want to implement the commission's verdict by force, a new ecclesiastical court was the only way out. Early in 314, the emperor sent out letters convening a synod of bishops from all his provinces. This time, it was to be held in southern Gaul, in Arelate, and presided over by the bishop of that city. The date for the start of the session was set for August 1. The text of the summons has been preserved in a letter from Constantine to the bishop of Syracuse, Chrestos. Other invitations sent to other church dignitaries were undoubtedly identical in content.

---

[84] Abthugni was an ancient city in Roman North Africa near present day Suwar

The letter begins with a brief reminder of the nature of the dispute and the activities of the Roman commission, then continues:

> Some have forgotten their salvation and the honor due to the most enlightened doctrine, and they do not cease to harbor personal enmities even now and do not want to submit to the judgment already passed. They claim that too few have expressed their opinion [during the Lateran commission's deliberations] and that the deliberations have been carried out too hastily and passed judgment without examining all the evidence. The result of all this is that those who should manifest fraternal love parted ways in an ugly and even obnoxious manner, thus giving cause for mockery to people who have nothing in common with the holy religion. We, therefore, must try to make sure that what should have ceased immediately after the verdict of the commission now finally finds its end in the presence of many.
>
> We have, therefore, ordered bishops, in very great numbers, from various and sundry localities to assemble in the city of Arelate by August 1. We deem it necessary to instruct you to request of the illustrious Latronianus, the Sicilian corrector [overseer of certain cities], a permit to travel by the state post. Take with you two more men of inferior rank, whom you may choose at your discretion, and three footmen to serve you on the road. Present yourself on the appointed day at the above-mentioned town.[85]

The emperor also ordered authorities in Africa to investigate whether Felix had indeed given up the Holy Scriptures during the persecution. Protocols of these investigations and various other related documents have been preserved. The material is fascinating, as it sheds light on the relations within the Christian communities of the time. Some of the Donatists, wishing to destroy Felix at all costs, committed fraud and forgery that were downright brazen. The outcry of one of the city officials, a pagan, summarized the whole affair. "So, this is the honesty of Christians!" sounds particularly derisive.

As far as we can infer from the materials available today, Felix

---

[85] Eusebius X 5

was completely innocent. The synod of Arelate—thirty-three bishops participated—not only repeated but even tightened the stipulations of the Lateran commission. Indeed, it stated in its decision that even ordinations made by a *traditor*-bishop remained valid. The members of the synod also condemned the Donatist doctrine in a letter to the bishop of Rome. He was then one Sylvester, the successor of Miltiades. Sylvester had been represented in Arelate by two envoys. The letter describes Caecilianus's opponents as insolent people who could neither present their case properly nor support their accusations with evidence.

The synod also enacted a number of provisions concerning church discipline. From the point of view of the relationship between the church and the state, the two most interesting are the following: one allows Christians to hold higher offices, even governorships, but at the same time places them under the special supervision of local bishops; the other prohibits Christian soldiers, under the penalty of excommunication, from leaving military ranks in peacetime.

The emperor watched the proceedings closely; it is even possible that he was in Arelate at the time. He probably sent some sort of address to the synod, but the surviving document, which claims to be such a letter, is, in fact, a later forgery or, at best, an inept alteration of the original. One thing is beyond any doubt: the emperor grew weary of long, petty ecclesiastical disputes. This is conclusively proven by the final sentence in the synod's letter to Pope Sylvester. It reads briefly but eloquently:

> Finally, the disheartened [emperor] ordered everyone to return to their dioceses.

For Constantine was faced with political decisions of a far greater importance.

Constantine in Trier

Our outline of the Donatist affair in 312-314 might give the impression that Constantine was interested almost exclusively in the issues of the Church during this time. This would be wrong. We were able to present the problem of Donatism and the Emperor's attitude to it very extensively for the simple reason that we have a considerable body of contemporary literature on the subject at our disposal. This is due to the Christian writers of the time, who devoted much attention to the African schism. Of course, Constantine had to deal with the issue only because of its possible political consequences. If we had accurate reports of the emperor's daily preoccupations, we would certainly find that other matters were of much greater concern to him.

As we remember, Constantine left Italy soon after his talks with Licinius in Milan, probably in April 313. From then on, he resided in Gaul, in Trier. That city was then the true capital of the West. Directly upon his arrival, the Emperor first crushed the Franks on the lower Rhine, then developed an energetic legislative activity.

It is difficult to present in more detail the considerable number of edicts, rescripts, and mandates that almost certainly date to this period. They concern a wide variety of matters; they regulate property and economic issues, define the relationship between freedmen and their former lords, regulate administrative and judicial proceedings. Regarding the last area, it is worth noting the decree on the correct mode of appeal from the judgments of the lower instances to the emperor. In the document, Constantine confesses frankly that he wished to limit appeals so as not to interrupt his other work. As early as the autumn of 313, an important edict appeared, freeing Christian clergy from all burdens to the state; this seems to be an extension of the same provision, which, as we recall, had been in force in the African provinces since the spring of 313 with respect to all clergy loyal to Caecilianus. At the same time, the emperor also freed palace functionaries (*palatines*) from the same burdens.[86]

In a state as bureaucratic to the core as the Empire was at the time, the inner workings of the complex machinery required the ruler's constant attention. But at the same time, developments in the other eastern part of the theoretically single empire had to be closely monitored, for from there could come either a deadly danger or a welcome opportunity for new conquests. It seems that at the time of the Synod of Arelate, a great and irreconcilable conflict began to unfold between Constantine and Licinius.

The First Conflict with Licinius

The sequence of events of 314-316 is unclear, as our sources are fragmentary and sometimes contradictory. The chronology is particularly difficult, and we will yet return to it, but let us present the general outline of events first.

In February 313, in Milan, Licinius married Constantine's half-sister Constantia; the two rulers took the opportunity to discuss the most important affairs of the Empire. Some evidence suggests that they agreed to maintain the old system of tetrarchy, and it seems that Constantine was prepared to give up direct rule over Italy. This sounds paradoxical: why, then, did he set out against Maxentius in the first place? Yet, it does make sense. First, Italy would have remained in Constantine's sphere of influence, for the authority there would have almost certainly gone to the husband of his half-sister, Anastasia, a certain Bassianus, who would have ruled as his Caesar. Constantine would have settled him in Rome all the more gladly since he liked neither the city nor Italy in general. This is evidenced by the fact that during his entire reign, from 312 to 337, he stayed in the capital on the Tiber only three times, each time very briefly. But he gladly stayed in Gaul and later in the Balkan provinces.

---

[86] C. Th. XVI 2, 2; C. Th. VI 36, 1

The putative future lord of Italy found favor and acceptance with Licinius, for Bassianus's brother, Senecio, was among the highest-ranking dignitaries of his entourage. Thus, the project seemed close to realization. But it was thwarted unexpectedly and under very dramatic circumstances. Unfortunately, we don't know the details. We do not even know which of the rulers overturned the agreement that had already been reached. Sources contradict each other. Some state that Licinius managed to involve Bassianus in some plot; the conspiracy was detected, and the traitor was put to death on the orders of Constantine. Others claim that Licinius bore no blame in the affair, that Constantine reneged on the terms of the settlement, and even tried to wrest certain border territories from Licinius. Knowing what we know about Constantine, this latter version seems more likely. Constantine was certainly concerned about Licinius's increased power now that he had acquired the rich eastern provinces. In the new situation, giving up Italy would have been reckless; on the contrary, common sense dictated that Licinius's power should be undermined—and as soon as possible.

A war broke out. It was fought in the Balkans, which suggests that Constantine was the attacking party. For the first time, the armies of the two emperors clashed on the battlefields near the city of Cibalae; it was located in the lands of present-day Serbia, between the Sava and the Danube. After a day-long and very bloody battle, Licinius retreated under the cover of darkness. The second battle took place in Thrace, today's Bulgaria, near that country's current border with Turkey. The armies of Licinius and Valens—Valens had been the commander of the Danube legions and Licinius raised him to the dignity of Caesar—stood bravely but began to give way at the end of the day. With the fall of night, the eastern commanders withdrew their forces. Anticipating that the victorious Constantine would immediately move against Byzantium, they stepped aside. Indeed, Constantine did attempt to push forward but had to stop almost immediately, as it was reported that the enemy was approaching from the flank. In this situation, and taking into account the fatigue of his army, Constantine agreed to negotiations.

The peace agreement stipulated that Constantine would acquire all the Balkan provinces except the eastern parts, that is, Thrace and Moesia. Valens was to be put to death, and to show to all that a full agreement had been reached, Constantine and Licinius assumed the traditional office of consuls as of the new year.

When did these incidents take place? It is known for certain that the Battle of Cibalae was fought on October 8, but of what year? Until recently, it was generally accepted that the entire campaign began and ended in the autumn of 314. This assumption was based on some interpretations of some ancient sources and the fact that Licinius and Constantine were consuls in 315. Recently, however, it has been argued on the basis of some numismatic data that the war must have been fought later, in 316. In that case, the joint consulate of the two emperors would have preceded the outbreak of the conflict. Finally, there is another view: that there were two wars; the first ended in 314 with the Battle of Cibalae and was followed by the joint consulate in 315, and a second war in 316, with the Battle of Thrace and the final peace settlement.[87]

One way or the other, Valens was murdered.

The Triumphal Arch

On July 21, 315, Constantine arrived in Rome to celebrate his so-called *decennalia*—the tenth anniversary of his reign. As we recall, the military hailed Constantine as Augustus in Britain on July 25, 306; by Roman custom, that year was counted as the first.

Arriving in Rome, the emperor was finally able to see the triumphal arch, the erection of which had been voted by the Senate back in 312 to celebrate his victory over Maxentius. After three years of work, the monument was almost ready. It has survived only slightly

---

[87] About the chronology of these events, see P. Bruun, *Studies in Constantine Chronology*, New York 1961; R. Andreotti, *Licinius*, in *Dizionario Epigrafico di Antichita Romane*.

damaged to this day. It remains one of the most beautiful and best-known monuments of ancient Rome.

The capital of the empire had once been decorated with dozens of triumphal arches. Only three remain. Two stand along the Via Sacra, which runs through the Roman Forum: the Arch of Titus, commemorating the conquest of Jerusalem in AD 70, and the Arch of Septimius Severus, dating to AD 203; while the monument to Constantine was built along the Via Triumphalis, between the Celius and the Palatine, near the Colosseum.

The structure is twenty-one meters high. It consists of three arches, the middle one eleven meters high, the two side arches seven meters each. Above the central arch there is an inscription which proclaims why the Senate and the people worship the emperor, the chastiser of the tyrant, the liberator of the city, the builder of peace. We have already discussed the term *instinctu divinitatis,* appearing in this inscription. The entire monument is richly decorated with columns, statues, and bas-reliefs. However, research has shown conclusively that many parts of the decoration are not original: they were transferred from other, earlier buildings of Imperial Rome. Obviously, such a procedure greatly sped up the work and reduced costs. The eight statues above the columns were taken from the Forum of Trajan. The eight circular medallions above the side arches came from some monument of Hadrian's time. The reliefs above the arches were taken from Marcus Aurelius's triumphal arch.

But some ornaments were made especially for the arch. We should say at once that they are artistically inferior to the earlier works, although they are obviously important for our understanding of the period. Particularly interesting is the lower frieze above both side arches, depicting scenes from Constantine's life: his deeds when he fought alongside Galerius in Asia, his triumphs over the Franks and the Alamemanni, his victory over Maxentius, his speech to the people in the Forum. Also important for their symbolism are the medallions on the side walls. One depicts a moonset, the other a sun rising in a chariot. The last, as we already said, has religious meaning.

Sylvester

In Rome, the emperor met the new bishop of the city, Sylvester, for the first time. Sylvester had assumed this ecclesiastical office after Miltiades in 314. He was to hold it for a long time, until 335. Thus, his pontificate almost fully coincided with the reign of Constantine, which lasted until 337. However, while we know a lot about the life and politics of the emperor, the pope remains a shadowy figure. Our sources speak of him rarely and sparsely, incomparably less than they do of other prominent bishops of the period. Apparently, he was not a strong or interesting personality. We know that he was born in Rome; that he was laid to rest in the church he built near the catacombs of Priscilla; that at the Synod of Arelate and later at the Council of Nicaea, he acted not in person but through his envoys. On the other hand, the name of this pope is among the best-known today because, after his canonization, his holiday in the liturgical calendar was set for December 31, which is why, in many European languages, New Year's Eve is also called "Sylvester."

Since we know so little about him, his legend seems all the more important. Later centuries could not accept that two men, each other's contemporaries, powerful Christians in a period so important for the future fate of Christianity, were practically strangers. Gradually, a fantastic tale arose in various versions, reaching its final shape only at the end of the fifth century. Here is its basic outline:

Constantine and his wife had initially persecuted Christians, and very harshly, too. Pope Sylvester had to flee Rome. Meanwhile, the emperor fell ill with leprosy. Pagan priests advised him to bathe in a pool filled with the blood of children. However, apostles Peter and Paul appeared to the sick man in a dream and ordered him to summon Sylvester, who knew the right medicine for his sickness. This is what happened. Sylvester laid his hands on the emperor's head, ordered him to perform seven days of penance, then blessed the water in the palace pond. After bathing in it, the emperor saw Christ and was completely healed. From then on, he was a Christian. He publicly testified to his conversion, showed great favor to his fellow Christians, and began the construction of two churches: one of them on the grounds of the Lateran Palace and the other in the Vatican, over the tomb of the Apostle Peter. He notified his mother, then residing in Nicomedia, of everything. She, however, was reluctant to hear the news, as she herself leaned towards the Jewish religion. In view of this, Constantine asked her to come to Rome and bring her rabbis. Here, a disputation with Christian priests took place in the presence of Constantine and Helena, and among the arbitrators sat a pagan philosopher. The great theological dispute ended with Helena and her Jewish rabbis admitting defeat and the truth of the Christian revelation and accepting baptism.

The legend—there is no need to demonstrate its complete fiction— became a kind of fact itself since it influenced the ideas of many generations in the early Middle Ages. And this made possible one of the boldest and most consequential forgeries that the history of our continent has ever known. In the eighth or ninth century, a document was forged, a document most commonly called the "Donation of Constantine," although the actual title was *Constitutum Constantini*. In the first part of this document, presumably granted by Constantine, the emperor allegedly speaks in his own words, narrating how he was healed of a disease and how he received baptism at the hands of Sylvester. He then justifies his gratitude thereby and the fantastic endowment he is about to make in favor of the bishop of Rome and his successors, granting him primacy over all the churches of Christendom, including the great patriarchates of the East; dominion over Rome, Italy, and all the provinces, cities and towns of the West; the right to imperial insignia and honors; and the right to exclusive jurisdiction over all Christian clergy.

For the entire Middle Ages, this "donation" was taken seriously, even by the enemies of the papacy. Thus, the forgery played a significant role in the disputes and conflicts of the age, both political and ideological. That the document was a forgery was demonstrated only in the 15th century.

Meeting each other for the first time in the summer of the year 315, Constantine and Sylvester could in no way have predicted that the posterity would bring their names together in such a bizarre way.

Donatus Again

This time, too, Constantine stayed in Rome for a very short time. He arrived on July 21 and left by late September. By the beginning of October, he was already in Milan, where he stayed for some time, not very long; by January 316, we find him in Trier.

All these months—on the Tiber, on the Po, beyond the Alps— the emperor had to deal with the issue of Donatism. The provisions of the Arelate synod remained a dead letter; the disturbances in Africa continued. While Constantine was still in Rome, the Donatists continually harassed him with petitions, seeking permission to restore their bishops in Africa.

Constant pestering had only one effect—of making the emperor even more hostile to the dissident cause. But he was also angered by the opposing side, Caecilianus and his followers. For when he summoned the bishop of Carthage to appear in Rome, the latter ignored the invitation without offering an excuse. Outraged, the emperor began to show some consideration to the Donatists; he is said to have declared publicly that he would hand them victory in the dispute if they proved themselves right in even one instance. Meanwhile, the unexpected happened: some bishops, Donatist supporters all, fled from Rome to Africa. Furious, the emperor sent the rest under escort from Rome to Milan, where he himself soon arrived. From there, at the request of a high court official, he dispatched two bishops to Africa: they were to oversee the business on the spot and conduct the election of a new bishop of Carthage. The move shows that the emperor had had enough of the two warring factions. Donatus and Caecilianus remained under house arrest in Italy.

Alas, the dispatched bishops accomplished nothing. There were new riots in Carthage. Donatus managed to escape to Africa, and Caecilianus soon followed in his footsteps.

By then, the emperor was already in Trier. At the beginning of 316, he toyed around with the idea of going to Carthage in person. He even freed some Donatists whom he had interned; this was undoubtedly intended to create a favorable atmosphere prior to his arrival in Africa. And in a letter sent to the governor of Africa, Constantine announced:

> When I arrive, my clear judgment will show in the most obvious possible way both to Caecilianus and to his opponents how the Supreme Deity should be worshipped and what worship suits Him best.[88]

These words prove conclusively that by now, Constantine treated Catholics and Donatists almost equally. They also show that the emperor considered himself entitled to interfere in all the internal affairs of Christianity, regardless of the verdict of the synods of bishops. In the aforementioned letter, he cites neither the Lateran Synod nor the Synod of Arelate. The quoted sentence is, in fact, a blatant declaration of *Caesaropapism,* and in its purest form: for no longer only matters of personnel and organization, but even the manner of worship is to be determined by the temporal ruler. For Constantine, only political considerations were important. Order in Africa had to be restored at all costs. If Christians failed to do it by themselves, he, the emperor, responsible before the "Supreme Deity"

---

[88] W. H. C. Frenc, *The Donatist Church,* p. 157 footnote 7

for the affairs of the entire Empire, would accomplish it by the power of his authority.

And then there was a change. It is difficult to say what caused it. On November 10, 316, while staying in Milan, the emperor notified the governor of Africa that he considered Caecilianus completely correct and his opponents vicious slanderers. And a few months later, in the spring of 317, orders went out to suppress the schism by force: the Donatist churches should be confiscated and their bishops exiled.

Constantine's policy concerning the African religious conflict has been and continues to be the subject of harsh criticism from historians. Indeed, it does not bring honor to the emperor as a statesman. It is characterized by a lack of consistency, volatility, and vacillation. One can try to find some justification for his conduct, but whatever that may be, it only deepened the schism within African Christianity, exposed Roman rule in Africa to many difficulties, and contributed to the growth of similar conflicts elsewhere.

Constantine in Serdica

Constantine remained in Gaul until the summer of 316; first in the north, in Trier, then in the south, in Arelate. It was there, in Arelate, probably in August, that Fausta gave him a son. He was named after his father, and to avoid confusion, he is called Constantine II or Constantine the Younger. He was not the emperor's first-born son, for Crispus had been born about ten years earlier; Constantine had him with Minervina, his illegitimate wife, whom he had to dismiss when he married Fausta.

In the early autumn of 316, the emperor crossed the Alps and arrived in northern Italy. He headed east, through Milan and Verona, toward the Balkan provinces. On December 4, we note his presence in Serdica, present-day Sofia. What was the reason for this journey? Why did the emperor abandon Gaul and rush towards the eastern reaches of his dominion despite the unpropitious season? It seems that a new war with Licinius broke out in the autumn of 316. As we recall, until recently, it was traditionally assumed that the first war between the two Augustuses took place in the autumn of 314; both the Battle of Cibalae and the war operations in Thrace were thought to have happened in that short period. However, some clues suggest that we should separate these two battles; that the battle of Cibalae was fought on October 8, 314; was followed by a peace settlement which gave Constantine most of the Balkans; then both emperors assumed the consulship for 315. Then, in the autumn of 316, there was a new conflict and a second defeat of Licinius, this time in Thrace. The immediate reason for the second clash is not known, but it is easy to guess that in an atmosphere of mutual suspicion, even a minor incident could have had dangerous consequences. It is possible that this time, the fault lay with Licinius, eager to regain lost territory and gathering his armies for this purpose. Some believe that he elevated the commander of his troops in Moesia, Valens, to the dignity of Caesar only in 316.

The peace concluded at the end of 316 confirmed Constantine's territorial acquisitions of 314 and may have given him some more territory in western Thrace. Licinius thus only held on to the Black Sea coast of the peninsula. Moreover, he agreed to the execution of his just-appointed co-ruler, Valens, who ended up being blamed for the whole affair.

In return, however, Licinius, too, received some concessions.

On March 1, 317, Constantine proclaimed a new system of co-government at Serdica. Both of Constantine's sons were elevated to the dignity of Caesars: the roughly twelve-year-old Crispus and the several-month-old Constantine II. But so was the several-year-old son of Licinius, called Licinianus, who had already borne this title in the East since 314, though without Constantine's consent. We do not know what territorial division of the Empire was envisaged. For the time being, in view of the minority of all three Caesars, this had no practical significance. Thus, while the system introduced by Diocletian seemed to revive, it was nevertheless given a completely different meaning, for the right to inherit the throne was elevated to the rank of a governing principle.

The Homecoming

Starting with the autumn of 316, Constantine remained in the Balkan provinces for eight years, until the summer of 324. He left only once, in 317, to spend a few months in northern Italy. During these eight years, he changed his place of residence several times. He resided most in Serdica, today's Bulgarian-Sophia. But at least as often, he stayed in Sirmium. This town is now called Sremska Mitrovica and is located on the Sava, about fifty kilometers south of Belgrade, Serbia. Constantine also visited the city where he was born, Naissus, present-day Serbian Niš. But he was not at all interested in Greece: the southernmost city where we find him is Thessalonica, today's Saloniki.

The fact that he moved his residence to the Balkans for such a long period is striking. It can be explained in various ways. Certainly, the danger from the Goths played a significant role. We know that Constantine strengthened the fortifications in some of the border areas at the time and fought off raiding parties trying to cross the Danube. But there is also a suggestion that Constantine was simply attached to the territory from his boyhood years. So, when he finally regained them, he bid farewell to the gentle charm of fertile northern Gaul and the enchanting beauty of Provence. He remained loyal to the Balkans until the end of his days; indeed, he later established his new capital at a place where the peninsula met Asia Minor.

During those eight years, from 316 to 324, Constantine conducted an almost feverish legislative activity. Of the approximately three hundred and fifty legislative acts issued under his name, nearly one hundred and fifty are from this period. And yet, this is certainly only a fraction of the edicts, rescripts, and constitutions that came out of the imperial chancellery at the time. They concerned the administration of justice, civil and property law, and administrative procedures. Without going into details, we should point out the main thrust of this legislation.

And so, above all, we see the desire to defend the lower classes from exploitation by the mighty, although clear status differences between the estates are upheld. For example: for raping a girl or seizing another's property, even a Senator should be tried immediately without notifying the emperor. On the other hand, a union between a free man and a slave was to be considered illegal and dishonorable; their children were slaves. In certain cases, if the slave is someone else's property and the man living with her belongs to the estate of the *decurions*, that is, to the upper stratum of the bourgeoisie, very severe punishments are prescribed: she is to be sentenced to work in the mines, while he is to be deported to an island and forfeit all his property.

Constantine was a simple man and generously applied harsh punishments. Thus, for example, child traffickers had hitherto been thrown into the mines, but now the emperor decided that if a slave or a freedman committed the crime, he was to be thrown to the wild beasts during games; if he was a free man, he was to fight in the circus as a gladiator, but the thing should be so arranged that he should die without fail. Death was even prescribed to those creditors who, to settle an unpaid debt, seized oxen used for plowing or slaves working the land; for such seizures, the emperor pointed out, caused delays in the payment of tribute to the state.

However, relatively humanitarian provisions are also found in Constantine's laws. He forbids the branding of criminals on the face, motivating it by the fact that the human face is shaped "in the image of heavenly beauty:" legs or hands should be branded instead. He recommends that prisoners under investigation should not be shackled too tightly or held in dungeons but should be brought out into the sunlight at dawn each day.[89]

In parallel with this legislative activity, Constantine vastly expanded the clerical control apparatus and introduced an increasingly strict tax regime—for Constantine had to constantly reinforce his

---

[89] C. Th. IX, 1, 1; XII 1, 6; IX 18, 1; IX 30, 1; IX 40,2; IX 3,1

troops as he prepared for the final showdown with Licinius.

The Reign of Licinius

Ancient writers paint Licinius and his rule in the darkest possible colors; they call him cruel, a miser, a tyrant, a debauchee. Eusebius of Caesarea is the most eloquent:

> He issued a law saying that no one was allowed to manifest human feelings toward starving prisoners by giving them food; that no one was allowed to show pity to those who were groaning in chains and starving to death; that no one was allowed to be charitable, and that to do charity was forbidden even to those whose nature was inclined to compassion. This was undoubtedly one of the most ruthless and cruel laws, punishing the very sense of pity.
>
> Why even mention his new marriage laws or his new ideas concerning the dying, by which he dared to abolish the excellent and wise old Roman laws and, in their place, establish something barbaric and cruel!
>
> In addition, he came up with a thousand charges against his subjects, frequent seizures of gold and silver, new ways of reassessing the land, and even penalties imposed on villagers, who had long since died. How many people, including those completely innocent, did this enemy of mankind condemn to exile! How many men of illustrious lineage and great gravitas did he lock up in prison and divorce them from their wives in order to give them to his hideous servants to dishonor! With how many wealthy women and young virgins did this worn-out old man use in drunken madness to satisfy his unbridled lust! Why drag all this out when his last antics prove how small and insignificant his first crimes were![90]

Of course, Eusebius can hardly be considered an impartial witness. Today, scholars are inclined to temper the harsh judgment of the ancients, and while it is difficult to deny that Licinius had many vices,

---

[90] Eusebius X, 7

and the full list of his crimes would certainly be long, he also had some merits as a ruler. He was not so much miserly as frugal: he tried to keep military expenditures within reasonable limits. In this respect, he was the opposite of Constantine, who paid his soldiers generously but did so at the expense of the population. Licinius also undertook strenuous efforts to uphold the traditional iron discipline in his legions.

No doubt he targeted the rich. But he confiscated their estates not only for the sake of his treasury but also to help the declining cities and the rural poor. One ancient writer puts it bluntly: "He was helpful to commoners and peasants because he had grown up among them."[91]

In one case, however, one must admit that his critics were absolutely right: Licinius was an uncouth and uneducated man. He had an almost pathological hatred of high culture and its bearers, the intelligentsia, which he called "the poison and blight of social life." He especially despised lawyers, for they, trained in the tradition of Roman rule of law, could not accept his decisions.[92]

But Licinius faced his greatest difficulties in the religious sphere.

The Rise of Arianism

The great moral issue of how to deal with priests who had apostatized during the persecution led to violent disputes among Christians not only in North Africa but also in Egypt. And just as in Africa, also here, on the Nile, these disputes were further fueled by personal animosities. They involved increasingly wider circles, finally resulting in a large-scale, long-lasting split.

In Egypt, the main proponent of strict rejection of the "fallen priests" was Melitios, bishop of Lycopolis. He began his campaign as early as 305-306. He expelled priests whom he considered unworthy and ordained others in their place. He did this even in Alexandria,

---

[91] *Epitome de Caesaribus*, 41, 8
[92] Ibid., 41, 9

although the bishop there, Peter, recommended leniency and forbearance and, occupying a see which, according to tradition, had been founded by the apostle Mark, was regarded as the head of the whole church of Egypt.

Accused of indiscipline and inciting violence, Melitios was finally excommunicated. But then a new wave of persecution came. The bishop of Lycopolis and many of his followers were deported to Palestine and sentenced to hard labor in the mines. They returned to Egypt only in the wake of Galerius's Edict of Toleration in 311 and immediately resumed their former attacks on the "fallen priests." In the autumn of that year, Maximinus Daza unleashed a new wave of persecution, and bishop Peter died a martyr's death. This made such a huge impression that many of Melitios's former associates, among them a certain priest named Arius (*Areios* in Greek), broke with him and returned to the bosom of the mainstream community. Nevertheless, Melitian communities persisted. They lasted for generations and centuries; it seems that they only died out in the eighth century. This is all the more noteworthy because Melitios did not put forward any specific theological doctrine. In essence, his whole movement boiled down to personal issues. We saw an identical situation in Africa when we discussed the rise of Donatism.[93]

For all its similarities with Donatism, Melitianism was a much weaker movement. Yet, its historical significance proved far greater because the general sense of indiscipline within the church fomented by Melitios prepared the ground for the formation of a new, widespread, and lasting split—the church will call it a heresy—that was to have an enormous impact on the subsequent fate of both Christianity and the entire empire.

The origin of the heresy is linked to the person of Arius. We know relatively little about the man himself. He was born shortly after 250, probably somewhere in Libya. He received a thorough education; for some time, he studied in Antioch in Syria at the famous theological

---

[93] Re Militios, see H. I. Bell, *Jews and Christians in Egypt*, Oxford 1924, 39-99

school of Lucian, who, in turn, had been a pupil of various teachers of Platonic philosophy. Later, Arius held a priestly office in Alexandria, where he attained the dignity of presbyter in one of its largest churches.[94] He enjoyed great respect as an ascetic and great popularity as a preacher, especially among women. His appearance alone made a great impression, for he was a tall, gaunt man with a serious though angelic face.

A man named Alexander became the new head of the Egyptian church. Melitios fought him as he had previously fought Peter, but about 319, he approached the bishop of Alexandria with the complaint that Arius's sermons, which attracted great crowds of listeners, expressed views contrary to Church teaching. Why did Melitios make this accusation? He may have wanted to take revenge on Arius for abandoning him a dozen years earlier; but perhaps he also wished to publicize that the supposedly orthodox tolerated a heretic in their midst.

Alexander investigated the matter. He concluded that Arius indeed professed and propagated a doctrine that deviated from the traditional teaching of the Church. This doctrine—the nucleus of Arianism—boiled down to a thesis that went something like this: only God the Father is eternal and uncreated; Christ, the *Logos* or Word, called into being by the Father out of nothing, could not possibly be equal to Him and was thus at best the first and special work of God.[95]

Arius was excommunicated, which he naturally protested. A synod of nearly a hundred Egyptian and Libyan bishops met in Alexandria and upheld the excommunication almost unanimously. Arius deemed it safer to leave Egypt. He decided to seek support elsewhere. In Palestine, our old acquaintance, Eusebius, bishop of Caesarea, received him rather favorably. But Arius found a truly devoted ally only in Asia Minor, in Nicomedia. The bishop of that city, also named Eusebius, had once been his colleague during their

---

94 In the ancient Near Eastern church this was a priestly rank considered equal to that of a bishop.

95 Re Arianism, see S. Rogala, *Die Anfange des arianischen Streites*, 1907

studies in Antioch; hence, their friendship and their similarity of views. Thanks to his influence at the court of Constantia, wife of Licinius, Eusebius convened a synod that overturned the Alexandrian decision and demanded that Arius and his followers be restored to their church offices. But when Arius returned to Egypt, the conflict flared up again with redoubled intensity. Ingenious and energetic, Arius did not hesitate to propagate his views among the faithful, resorting even to the modern marketing techniques of rhymes and doggerel songs.

Thus, the issue continued to fester. Thanks to Arius's vigorous marketing and the strenuous efforts of Eusebius of Nicomedia, the dispute spread beyond the borders of Egypt. Almost all the bishops of the East were obliged to take sides. Since various means of popular agitation were used, doctrinal issues soon became a matter of interest for the wider masses.

We may be surprised today that such an abstract doctrinal issue managed to provoke such heated reactions, but there was a reason for this phenomenon. In Egypt, passions elicited by the Melitian dispute had not yet calmed down. As happened elsewhere, seemingly purely theological debates brought out various ethnic and economic conflicts that had accumulated within the community over the generations. Finally, the dispute also had its deeper roots, for it was also a rebellion of the Greek way of thinking, imbued with the old philosophical culture, against the vague, imprecise, and deliberately irrational notions that dominated the system of Christian theology of the time.

The Religious Policy of Licinius

In the course of these events, and partly as a result of them, Licinius began to change his attitude toward Christianity.

We have seen how vehemently Eusebius condemned this emperor in his *History of the Church*. He condemned him as a persecutor and, full of holy indignation, quoted the following facts: Licinius expelled all Christians from his court; removed from the army or demoted soldiers and officers who refused to make sacrifices to pagan gods; he treated bishops harshly, and some of his overzealous governors even put them to death. Finally, Eusebius states with all conviction that the emperor intended to initiate a universal persecution against the faithful.

Eusebius' account is blatantly biased and does not deserve to be taken at face value. However, we cannot deny the fact, attested to by other sources as well, that at a certain moment, Licinius began to show a clear dislike for Christians and issued a series of decrees detrimental to them. And yet it was the same Licinius whose troops had recited a prayer to "the Supreme God" before the decisive battle with Maximianus Daza; the same Licinius who, shortly after entering Nicomedia, proclaimed toleration and a return of seized church property and who, in 314, earned praise from the lips of Eusebius as one of the guardians of the Church. So, when and why did such a sharp about-turn in his policy occur?

The context of Eusebius's narrative suggests that this happened after the emperor lost the Balkan provinces, perhaps around 320. This is confirmed by references in other authors as well and must mean that new factors appeared on the political scene, factors which Licinius had to take into account in his policy-making. First of all, Constantine began to show friendship and protection to Christians, issuing a whole series of laws in that spirit. This gave rise to the suspicion that the ruler of the West wanted to win over the Church, so powerful in the East, in preparation for the final showdown for control of the whole Empire. Eusebius informs us that Constantine enjoyed popularity among Eastern Christians. In this situation, Licinius had only two choices: either to outdo his colleague in favoring them or to seek to curb their influence. The first option was effectively closed to him, for Constantine had gone so far in his pro-Christian policy that Licinius, wishing to give something more, would probably have had to recognize the Church as an equal partner and agree to the existence of a state within a state. And therefore, Licinius took the opposite tack. He decided that his court, armies, and administration had to be purged of potentially hostile elements. He banned bishops' synods, making it very difficult for the Church to undertake coordinated action. He also sought to halt the march of Christianity by placing obstacles in the way of its missionary activity. And thus, for example, henceforth, only women were allowed to give religious instruction to women, and even bishops were forbidden to do so; and Christian services were allowed only outside of city walls.

There were no general bloody persecutions. If any executions did take place, they happened on the orders of an over-eager governor or two.[96]

Undoubtedly, the recent infighting within the Church also influenced Licinius's policies, for the Arian movement caused considerable public unrest. The emperor feared that riots could escalate into an open rebellion. His ban on synods was, in part, designed to prevent the conflict from deepening.

But Licinius's new religious policy only made Constantine all the more zealous in continuing his pro-Christian line.

The Day of the Sun

Constantine's edict of 321 declares:

> The venerable day of the Sun [*venerabilis dies Solis*] should be free from court trials and from all labor of the urban population; while the villagers can freely cultivate on this day because it often happens that the most favorable moment for plowing the land or planting vines falls on this day; so one should not lose the opportunity given by heavenly providence.[97]

And in a rescript dated July 21 of that year, the emperor explains:

> Although it seems inappropriate to disturb the venerable day of the

-----

96 Eusebius X 7
97 *Codex Justinianus*, III 12

Sun with disputes and quarrels in the courts, it is desirable to allow useful and virtuous activities on this day. Thus, it is permitted to liberate slaves and to perform emancipation [that is, release children from paternal authority].[98]

It can be said without exaggeration that this edict remains in force in most countries of the world to this day; for this *dies Solis* is, of course, our Sunday. The emperor established it for the first time in history as an official and legally binding day of rest. All subsequent ordinances in various eras and countries have merely been a repetition or adaptation of the edict of 321. However, Constantine did not act entirely arbitrarily and did not establish a completely new practice. He merely sanctioned a state of affairs that had already existed.

To put this edict in its proper light, we should discuss briefly a broader issue: the origins of the week and of the names of its days.

The seven-day week has been in existence since time immemorial among various Semitic peoples in Mesopotamia and Palestine. We all know that the god of the Jews forbade all work on the seventh day of the week: the Sabbath. Individual days of the Semitic week did not have names, they were only numbered. The Greeks knew no equivalent to the Semitic week, while the Roman week, called *nundinae*, had eight days: on its eighth day, free from farm work and schooling, markets were held.

It follows that our seven-day week comes from the Semitic practice, most likely via the Jews. Its introduction happened very slowly, proceeding from east to west, and was largely facilitated by Jewish colonies, numerous in various cities. In the first century of the new era, the seven-day week was already very well known, even in the West.

At the same time, another process took place: the individual days of the week acquired names derived from the names of the planets. Five were known at the time, and to them, the Moon and the Sun were added to make seven. This idea probably originated in the second century B.C. somewhere in the Near East; it spread very quickly

---

[98] C. Th. II 8, 1

178

thanks to the great esteem in which astrology was held. In the imperial era, the following names came into use in the western provinces: *dies Lunae, dies Martis, dies Mercurii, dies Jovis, dies Veneris, dies Saturni, dies Solis.* These names live on to this day in the Romance and Germanic languages. Just recall the French *lundi, mardi, mercredi, jeudi, vendredi.* Admittedly, instead of *dies Saturni* the name *Samedi*—from the Latin *dies Sabati*—was adopted in France; but in English, we have *Saturday* and designate *dies Solis* as *Sunday*—a faithful equivalent of the Latin. (Unlike the system prevalent in Western Europe, most Slavic nations count the days of the week: Tuesday is the Second Day, Wednesday the third, and so on. This naming convention is derived from Jewish practice).

And here is a noteworthy thing: Christians in the West continued to use the customary names of the days of the week, even though they sounded obviously pagan and astrological. But the Church was helpless in the face of a custom that had taken root too quickly and too deeply. Only in one case was there an attempt to change the name: instead of *dies Solis*, the term *dies dominica*, or the Lord's Day, was promoted, as on that day Christ was said to have risen, and Christian services were held to distinguish them from the Jews who worshipped on a Saturday. These efforts were partially successful; hence such names as Italian *domenica* or French *dimanche*.

By legally sanctioning *dies Solis* as a day of rest, Constantine undoubtedly acted with Christians in mind. However, there is nothing of the terminology of the new religion in his decree. Any worshipper of the Unconquered Sun could take the edict of 321 as evidence of the emperor's concern for the cult of that god.

The edict characterizes the deliberate and conscious ambiguity of Constantine's moves during this period. For while he is clearly acting in favor of the Christian cult, he does so in such a form and manner as not to alienate the followers of other cults. The same intentional ambiguity characterizes the emperor's other decrees during these years.

Edicts on Magic and Soothsaying

Probably very few of Constantine's legal decisions shed as much light on his religious ideas as his rescript of March 317 addressed to Bassus, Prefect of Rome. It contains provisions to the effect that:

> Punishable with the strictest penalties is the knowledge [*scientia*] of those who practice magic to harm human health or arouse love. On the other hand, one should not be punished if one resorts to such knowledge to cure a disease or prevent hail from destroying vines. For such actions do not bring harm to anyone's health, wealth, or good name, but on the contrary, they seek to protect them.[99]

In other words, the emperor took the skills of magicians and astrologers seriously. It would be difficult to find any Christian motivation in these decrees. They are really a continuation of similar laws issued by other emperors over the centuries. Magical and astrological practices were very widespread in all social classes, and everyone, including the emperors, was afraid to fall prey to them.

The edict of 319 goes further. In it, the emperor announced:

> No *haruspex* (fortune-telling priest) may enter another person's home, even that of friends. If he violates this prohibition, he will be burned alive, while those who host him will have their property confiscated and be themselves exiled to the islands. Whoever wishes to practice such superstition (*superstitio*) must perform its rites in public. Anyone who brings an accusation of the above offense is to be considered not an informer but a person worthy of reward.[100]

To fully appreciate the import of this edict, we should recall that the college of *haruspices* was one of the most ancient and venerable priestly organizations in Rome. Leading citizens were members, and the state formally consulted their advice on all unusual events ("omens"). Meanwhile, in an edict issued in the same year, 319, the emperor again threatened *haruspices*, priests, and their servants with punishment

---

99 C. Th. IX 16, 3

100 C. Th. IX 16, 1

should they dare to enter a private house, and adds:

> You who think it is profitable to engage in such outdated practices
> should visit the public altars and temples according to your custom,
> for we do not forbid the practice as long as it is performed in the
> open.[101]

It seems clear that while restricting pagan rites and rituals, the emperor
had Christianity in mind. Particularly noteworthy are the
contemptuous terms used in the law whenever traditional beliefs are
mentioned: "superstition," "outdated practice." It also seems that the
emperor feared that conspiracies might arise under the guise of private
religious services. This was especially true of Rome and its old
aristocracy, which was disinclined to embrace the ruler's pro-Christian
policies. The closing sentence of the first edict illuminates this aspect,
as it encourages informers to resume their activities: a stipulation
contradictory to the edict of 312, when immediately after entering
Rome, Constantine promised to end the "cursed plague of informers."

But here again is a surprising fact: about 320, lightning struck
the great Roman amphitheater now known as the Colosseum. Since
ancient custom dictated that in such cases, the college of *haruspices*
should be consulted regarding how such an omen should be
understood, the prefect of the city did so. He then forwarded their
opinion to the imperial court, to the head of the chancellery, who in
turn reported it to the ruler. Constantine's reply is preserved. In it, he
informs the prefect of Rome:

> If lightning strikes our palace or other public building, it is
> necessary, per the old custom, to ask the *haruspices* to explain the
> meaning of the omen. After such an opinion has been secured, it
> must be transmitted to us. Private persons may also follow this
> custom, as long as they do not do so in private, which is expressly
> forbidden.[102]

Thus, it is not clear what the emperor's views actually were at the time:

---

[101] C. Th. IX 16, 2

[102] C. Th. XVI 10, 1

he simultaneously favored Christians, venerated the day of the Sun, and took the skills of magicians and *haruspices* at face value.

Lactantius and Constantine

During this time, probably as early as 317, a figure already well-known to us entered Constantine's court: Lactantius, a professor of Latin literature and rhetoric at Nicomedia. He had been summoned there from Africa by Emperor Diocletian because of his reputation as a great scholar. Nevertheless, he did not achieve success in Nicomedia, as its Greek inhabitants were not very interested in his subject of study, and he lived in extreme poverty. However, he did not neglect his studies or writing. In those lean Nicomedian years, he wrote his most ambitious work, *Institutiones Divinae* ("The Divine Institutes"). It is a kind of presentation of the principles of Christianity but with a clear apologetic bent, addressing itself primarily to the *intelligentsia* of the time, that is, to the social stratum to which Lactantius himself belonged. The work is distinguished by its clarity of expression and beauty of language—its author is not called the Christian Cicero for nothing—but it is difficult to find much theological subtlety or interesting philosophical ideas in the work. Probably as a result of the popularity that the book gained among educated Christians, someone influential, perhaps Bishop Hosius, recommended Lactantius to the emperor. The latter was looking for tutors for his first-born son, Crispus. In choosing the rhetorician from Nicomedia, the emperor was certainly guided by practical considerations since Lactantius was one of the best Latin stylists of his times. However, selecting a Christian author carried obvious political overtones, even if the circle of imperial tutors also included supporters of traditional philosophical systems.

And so, fortune finally smiled on Lactantius, albeit at the very end of his life, for, born around 240, he was by then well over seventy. We know from a reference in one of the sources that upon his appointment, the writer left Nicomedia and went to Gaul. There—almost certainly in Trier—resided his pupil Crispus, administering the Gallic provinces in his father's name. Clearly, high officials and officers had a lot of say in running the business, for Crispus was only fourteen years old, but this did not prevent an orator from crediting him in a solemn speech with defeating the Germanic tribes on the Rhine.

While on the banks of the Moselle, Lactantius continued to work as diligently as he had previously done on the coast of Propontis. He completed the *Institutiones*, including a dedication to Constantine in both its preface and conclusion. He also published an abridgment of this great work and a separate treatise *De ira dei* ("On the Wrath of God"). For historians, however, the most valuable is his small booklet that we have used many times here: *De mortibus persecutorum* ("On the Deaths of the Persecutors"). The last political events mentioned in that work took place in 314, so it must have been written somewhat later, though it is difficult to determine when. Its voluble praises for Constantine and his father show that Lactantius was already associated with the family. On the other hand, we find no attacks on Licinius, which would indicate that the work was completed before that emperor initiated his new religious policy.

Liberations, Inheritance Rights, and Bishops' Courts

Bishop Hosius, whom we first encountered in connection with Donatism, continued to play an important role in Constantine's entourage. It is almost symbolic that he was the addressee of an important imperial decree dated April 18, 321, which declared:

> The act of liberating a slave, performed publicly in a church, is just as valid as one performed according to traditional legal rules. Members of the clergy can liberate their servants even without witnesses and by whatever formula they wish, also by testament.[103]

---

[103] C. Th. IV 7, 1

In July of that same year, a new law allowed the transfer of property to the Church via a testament.[104] Finally, the third law, issued perhaps a little earlier, allowed litigants to transfer a case, even one already begun, from secular tribunals to episcopal courts.[105]

The first two laws could be considered a logical application of the principle of tolerance, since by customary law, acts of liberation had been performed in pagan temples for centuries, especially in the East; and pagan temples had also had the unquestioned right to receive testamentary legacies. From a purely formal point of view, Constantine was thus granting Christians no more than equal rights. However, there was a fundamental and substantive difference: each pagan temple was essentially a separate entity and subject to the local authority like any other city institution. Whenever it so desired, the city or the *polis* freely regulated, controlled, and even disposed of temple property within its limits. However, the position of the Christian Church was different: it was an enormous, empire-wide institution with direct access to the highest echelons of power and dwarfing any and every local authority. And it was about to strike deep roots both legally and economically, creating independent structures parallel and equivalent to those of the state: a state within a state. Of course, it is also true that by virtue of these edicts, Christian communes assumed an increasing role in the burden of caring for the sick, orphans, poor, and the elderly, for many bequests were accompanied by such stipulations.

But the third decision, concerning bishops' courts, raises profound questions. The surviving text is not entirely clear, and neither is its date—perhaps it was AD 318. Another law of Constantine, dating to 333, seems to invoke this earlier one and interprets it very broadly: from now on, either party has the right—at any time during the trial—to request its transfer from the secular tribunal to a bishop's court, whose verdict would in practice be irrevocable. Perhaps, aware of the bureaucratism and corruption of the

---

[104] C. Th. XVI 2, 4
[105] C. Th. I 27, 1

184

secular tribunals, Constantine wished to bring relief to the poor and, at the same time, relieve his chancery from the prodigious mountain of appellate cases—since the episcopal courts would, as a result of the edict, become a kind of appellate instance. If so, these powers granted to bishops' courts so easily and generously—we could even say recklessly—failed to deliver on the expectations. Later emperors, ardent Christians themselves, issued a series of laws during the fourth and fifth centuries aimed at limiting the powers of the ecclesiastical judiciary.

Preparations for War

In 322, the Sarmatians, an Iranian nation sitting between the Danube and the Tisza in present-day Hungary, broke into the empire. Constantine crushed them, then crossed the great river, ravaged their country, and took many captives. The following year, the Goths, a Germanic nation of Scandinavian origin, crossed the lower Danube. Looting as they went, they overran the provinces of Moesia and Thrace. At the time, the emperor was in Thessalonica, where he oversaw the construction of a port and a navy. He immediately took to the field. He defeated the Goths and forced them to release thousands of captives. However, during this campaign, he crossed—intentionally or unintentionally—into Licinius's domains. The latter protested, but Constantine ignored him. Thus came the final rupture between the two.

That they were hostile to each other had been known for years throughout the empire and even beyond its borders; the bold attacks of the Sarmatians and Goths are best explained by nothing else. The clearest and commonly perceived indication of the swelling conflict was the matter of the consulates. The office had long been purely honorary. It was maintained as a respected relic of the republican past and a symbol of the unity of the Empire. The calendar was still dated with the names of the pair of consuls, changing every year. The emperors decided on the nominations and usually agreed amongst themselves in advance. They often held the consulate themselves, choosing a close associate or someone from their family members. But starting in 321, the provinces under the rule of Licinius no longer recognized the consuls appointed by Constantine; they refused to do so because the ruler of the West had broken a previous agreement by which Licinius and his son were to be consuls in 321. Instead, Constantine appointed his sons, Crispus and Constantine II.

It seems certain that Constantine wanted war and consciously tried to provoke it. His ultimate goal was the conquest of the entire Empire. He had nourished these plans for years, but from 320 on, he intensified his efforts. This was undoubtedly linked to events within the imperial family. In 317, Fausta gave birth to a second son; he was named after his grandfather, Constantius; in 320, a third son, named Constans, arrived. Thus, there were now four princes in the ruler's household.

It is quite understandable that Constantine was thinking about providing each of his sons with dominion over some part of the Empire. In this way, the tetrarchy would again be revived in the form that existed under Diocletian, but unlike Diocletian's, it would be tightly bound by family ties. In such an arrangement, of course, there would be no place for either Licinius or his son.

It is true that on March 1, 317, Constantine agreed to raise the young Licinius to the dignity of Caesar, but this happened a few months before Constantius was born on August 7 of that year and three years before the birth of Constans.

Starting in 321, both emperors began to build up their armies and prepare for war. Licinius began to repress Christians because he suspected them of favoring Constantine, while the latter redoubled his efforts to court the new religion. We can see this process reflected on the coins of the emperor of the West. Christian symbolism becomes more frequent and more explicit, while inscriptions in honor of the pagan deities disappear completely—except for one mint, a very important one, because located in Sirmium, that is, in one of Constantine's residences. That mint continued to strike coins glorifying the Unconquered Sun.

Hadrianopol, Byzantium, Chrysopolis

The sheer enormity of the armies testified to how carefully both sides had prepared for war. Licinius concentrated 150,000 foot soldiers and 15,000 horse in Thrace. Constantine's forces were slightly smaller at 130,000 men, including 10,000 horse. At sea, Licinius prevailed uncontested, for he had about 350 ships drawn from many lands, from Asia Minor to Egypt. Constantine would counter this armada with barely 200 ships. His main naval base was Piraeus, the port of Athens. He gave command of the fleet to his firstborn, Crispus, although he was barely twenty years old. The emperor himself took command of the land forces.

The civil war, one of the biggest and bloodiest ever to rock the Roman empire, began in the spring of 324. At the end of June, the two armies set up camp near Adrianople. They were separated by the River Hebrus, today's Maritsa, and neither side was eager to be the first to push through its swift current. Only after several days' standoff did Constantine manage to deceive the enemy with a trick and then surprise him with a bold attack: he crossed the river on horseback, surrounded by only twelve riders. Thus began, on July 3, a bloody battle that lasted until nightfall. The defeated Licinius retreated at nightfall to Byzantium. His scattered troops wandered through the surrounding wilderness. Gradually, most came over to Constantine's side.

Despite this disaster, Licinius's cause was not yet lost, for both the location and the powerful fortifications of Byzantium allowed for a long defense, especially since his control of the sea ensured a steady flow of reinforcements and supplies. Meanwhile, he would be able to raise new troops from the eastern provinces. In order to cope with the situation, Licinius appointed the highest official of his court, Martinian, as Augustus. Thus, he acted just as he had after his defeat a few years ago when he elevated Valens to the dignity of co-ruler. Both Augustuses stayed in Byzantium and successfully repelled the assailants. The besiegers built war machines and used various engineering measures that had been tried for centuries but failed to penetrate the city walls.

After several weeks of futile efforts, Constantine realized that the breakthrough had to be made elsewhere. He ordered Crispus, who was operating in the Aegean Sea, to force his way through the Hellespont. This seemed an impossible task, for a powerful fleet of Licinius stood in the strait. However, overconfident of its superiority, it did not take the necessary precautions; surprised by Crispus's deft maneuvering, it suffered heavy losses. The road to Byzantium stood wide open.

Licinius and Martinian had to change their plans. The most important thing now was to prevent Constantine from landing on the Asian coast, for this would have cut them off from their hinterland. Both Augustuses fled Byzantium but left troops behind to defend the city. Licinius established his quarters near Chalcedon and was to defend the Bosphorus crossing; Martinian left for Lampsacus to guard the Hellespont from there.

For some time, Licinius and Constantine conducted negotiations; in fact, they deceived each other and engaged in talks only to gain time. The former hastily gathered troops and soon had 130,000 men, including many barbarians who served as mercenaries, while the latter prepared for the crossing. In early September, Constantine managed to mislead his enemy again and landed on the Black Sea coast of the Chalcedonian Peninsula. Licinius immediately summoned Martinian. The decisive battle occurred on September 18 near the city of Chrysopolis. The opponents of Constantine, defeated again, took refuge behind the walls of Nicomedia. Byzantium surrendered at once.

Thanks to the mediation of Constance, the wife of Licinius and Constantine's half-sister, a deal was struck. Licinius and Martinian renounced all dignities, and in return, the victor swore a solemn oath that he would spare their lives. The former was sent to Thessalonica, while the latter was sent to eastern Asia Minor. A few months later, on the emperor's orders, both were murdered for alleged collusion with hostile barbarians. Licinius's son remained alive and even retained his private estate, a very considerable one, but a dozen years later, he too was murdered by Constantine.

Thus, after nearly forty years, the Empire again had only one master. But before we discuss his coming universal reign, we should try to understand the causes of his triumph.[106]

Gods and Armies

Ancient Christian writers, followed by various modern historians, put the issue simply and seemingly convincingly. They present the struggle between Licinius and Constantine as a clash of two religions: the cross, the symbol of the new faith, was victorious over polytheistic deities. Adopting such an interpretation, one would have to conclude that this was the first religious war in the history of Europe.

Eusebius of Caesarea, a contemporary of the events, seemed to see it in this light. He said as much, though in a veiled manner, in the brief afterword to his *History of the Church*, written after the defeat of Licinius. (There is some evidence that in an earlier edition of his work, Eusebius had treated the Eastern ruler rather forgivingly).

The aforementioned *Life of Constantine*, attributed to the same Eusebius, does not prevaricate. This hagiographic work was probably written in the second half of the fourth century and, therefore, well after the deaths of both Eusebius and Constantine. It is, therefore, at best, a rather free adaptation of a now-lost work by the bishop from Caesarea, if that. It is possible that from time to time, *Life* quotes authentic documents—we have no way of knowing. But even assuming as much, it is not easy to be sure that anything in it is not a fabrication. As a whole, it is a work of religious propaganda; it is meant

---

[106] Today's Üsküdar, an Asian suburb of Istanbul, Turkey

to show to future generations that the saintly ruler enjoyed the help of heaven at every turn.

We have already seen how *Life* described the matter of the symbol that had allegedly appeared to Constantine before the battle of the Milvian Bridge. That story is clearly a myth: the emperor is said to have seen a flag in the sky; he described its appearance to his goldsmiths; and on this basis, they created the *labarum*. However, the author apparently doubted whether this sounded believable. So, he asserted that he heard this account directly from Constantine's own lips. This *labarum* now returns again in the narrative of the war with Licinius, and the author again says he heard the story from the emperor:

> Constantine chose fifty men, distinguished by their courage and piety. Their task was to guard the holy standard; they were to surround it at all times and, during battle, take turns carrying it aloft. It happened once in the midst of a particularly bloody fight that an ensign, struck with fear, gave the banner to a comrade and stepped out of line himself as if to flee. At this point, he fell to the ground, mortally wounded. On the other hand, the one who carried the standard stood unharmed, although he was hit by arrows and bullets from all sides, but the missiles, by a miraculous coincidence, only hit the shaft of the banner. The same happened in later battles.[107]

The historical kernel of the legend is probably the fact that among the battle emblems of Constantine's army was indeed a *labarum*. In any case, a likeness of this sign is found on coins minted in Byzantium after 326.

The Life of Constantine resorts to an easy, stark contrast: on the one hand, a saintly and loving Christian, and on the other, a bloodthirsty pagan who summons priests and soothsayers all the way from Egypt, offers vain sacrifices to the deities, and in a programmatic speech before the start of hostilities proclaims himself the defender of the ancestral faith, trampled by the godless, and threatens to move

---

[107] *The Life of Constantine* II 7-9

against all "atheists" immediately after victory.[108]

And yet, the causes of the civil war had been political, not religious. All the motivation and symbolism so elaborated by Christian writers were of secondary importance. In fact, everything depended on the course of military operations and, therefore, on the efficiency of the two armies, and in both, the worshippers of the old gods still outnumbered Christians. Constantine won because he had armies that were more battle-hardened and better trained. He had an excellent recruiting base among the populations of the Danubian and Rhineland provinces, and it was easier for him to enlist Germanic mercenaries. And with his generosity, he won a loyal following of the legions. Meanwhile, the army of Licinius was dominated by a Middle Eastern element, not very resilient and not very brave, and with little sympathy for their leader, who was both harsh and frugal. Today, it is impossible to tell what effect the religious propaganda, so strenuously developed by Constantine, had. But it seems certain that it did not determine the course of events. However, it happened as it often does in history: what was only one means in the struggle for power rose in the eyes of later generations to the importance of the fundamental issue.

New Challenges

The great victor, Constantine, together with his son Crispus, the emperor most pleasing to God and his son completely like his father, took back their inheritance, restored the ancient unity of the Roman empire, brought under peaceful rule the whole land from the East to the last extremities of the West. Thus, the fear that once gnawed at them had now left the people. Wonderful celebrations and festive gatherings took place. Everything was as if flooded with a torrent of light, and those who had once felt benighted now looked at each

---

other with smiling faces and radiant eyes. Their festive pageants and songs glorified God, for so they had been taught, and the pious emperor, along with his God-loving children. Old misfortunes faded into oblivion, and all godlessness was forgotten. One lived by the present happiness and hoped for more which was yet to come. The victorious emperor's laws, full of graciousness, were posted everywhere, bearing evidence of his generosity and true piety.

Thus ended all tyranny, and only the unshakeable and just reign of Constantine and his children remained.[109]

Eusebius of Caesarea closes his *History of the Church* with these words. They sound beautiful, the fanfares of the final triumph—and yet how sarcastic and mocking some of these statements were to sound very, very soon.

It is quite understandable that a mood of jubilation prevailed among the population, not only the Christians. The end of the era of civil wars was a heartening event for all. A unified government heralded stability, and internal peace promised that the burden of armaments would soon decrease.

Constantine began his reign in the eastern provinces by canceling the orders of the "tyrant." His statues were toppled, and his and his son's names were erased from all inscriptions. Of course, all restrictions on the Christian communities were immediately revoked, again restoring and reiterating the edict of toleration. It even seems that some Christians, misunderstanding the attitude and intentions of Constantine, attempted to close pagan temples. The emperor's response to this was an edict calling for forbearance even toward those who still erred and denying that the tabernacles of pagan deities should be liquidated. The text of this edict has reached us only in a bizarre Christian reworking of *The Life of Constantine*. Its stylization and wording are of a kind that almost completely distorts the purpose of the original edict as a manifesto of broad tolerance.[110]

It was easy to revoke the laws of the "tyrant" but more difficult

---

[109] Eusebius X, 8
[110] *The Life of Constantine* II 48-60

to deal with the specific challenges that confronted the victor. Some of the solutions depended entirely on the ruler's will; these included the issue of the soldier's pay and the establishment of a new residence, while others proved beyond his control, even if he made great efforts towards their settlement.

Preparations for the Council

Following his victory in the autumn of 324, Constantine remained in Nicomedia, which he knew well from his youth. He was, however, intent on traveling further, as far as Syria and Egypt. Some preparations had already been made, but unexpectedly, the emperor changed his mind. He was stopped, it seems, by the news from Alexandria, where the religious conflict was reaching fever pitch. Constantine must have worried that he would be obliged to declare himself for either side soon upon his arrival in Egypt, which was something he was eager to avoid. He had given up visiting Africa years ago for the same reason. This time, too, he sent a deputy: his advisor, Bishop Hosius. The bishop carried a letter addressed to both sides. The letter, if the surviving text is to be believed, called for harmony and unity despite differences in doctrinal views: if philosophers can do this, how much more easily can the servants of God! The final words were forceful:

> Restore the peace of my nights and the cheer of my days so that I may henceforth enjoy the pleasure of a quiet life![III]

Hosius, of course, settled nothing. On the contrary, things seemed to reach a boiling point. The bishop returned deeply convinced that Alexander was right. Both Alexander and his opponent soon appeared in Nicomedia.

Again, the emperor acted similarly to the way he had acted in the matter of Donatus. He decided that it would be best to refer the

---

[III] *Life of Constantine* II 72

matter to an assembly of bishops. Arianism, however, differed in a very important way from the African schism, for it concerned doctrinal matters and was not limited to one land but touched Christian circles in all eastern provinces. It followed that one should not stop at convening a small group of bishops but should organize the deliberations of the largest possible number of church dignitaries. Thus –probably gradually—the idea was born to call a universal council, the first in the history of Christianity.

Its initiator and convener was the emperor. He issued respectful invitations to all the bishops. Originally, the convention was to meet in Ancyra—today's, Ankara. However, the ruler soon abandoned this intention and designated Nicaea, today's Iznik, a city near Nicomedia, as the meeting place. Allegedly, this was because of its better climate. In fact, we can easily guess that Constantine preferred that the deliberations take place where he could keep an eye on them.

The state covered the travel and room and board of all invitees, yet many refused to come. The "universal council" was really a convention of bishops from the eastern part of the Empire. Only a handful came from the West: one each from Africa, Italy, Gaul; Hosius can be considered to have represented Spain. Sylvester, bishop of Rome, excused himself by his old age; he sent two representatives. On the other hand, five bishops from outside the borders of the Empire showed up: two from Armenia, two from Crimea, and one from Persia. Tradition claims that three hundred and eighteen ecclesiastical dignitaries came to Nicaea. But clues in the sources suggest that only a little over two hundred did.

The Council of Nicaea

The first session was held on May 20, 325, in the great hall of the imperial palace. Constantine appeared in all the splendor of his majesty but without a bodyguard. Those gathered greeted him by rising and sat down only at a sign given by him. Then, the emperor gave a speech that sounded like a hymn in praise of the Church. It is difficult to know to what extent it expressed his personal views; it is probable that, like most official speeches in all times and in all countries, this one, too, was written by someone else, perhaps Hosius. There was no shortage of calls for unity. The emperor spoke in Latin, and only later did a secretary repeat his words in Greek.

In the course of two months of deliberations, Constantine made numerous appearances and sometimes took the chair. He also met with bishops individually. There were often violent disputes among the clerics, and each group tried to sway the ruler. Constantine was inundated with letters in which saintly men accused each other of the most vile misdeeds. He made no use of these materials but did not destroy them either. As long as the sessions lasted, he tried to maintain a semblance of impartiality, although it was obvious that he favored the orthodox bishop of Alexandria, Alexander—probably as a result of Hosius's persuasion.

If the council wanted to settle doctrinal issues, it had to formulate a precise confession of faith. The bishop of Caesarea, Eusebius, submitted his draft. It was considered too compromising, however, and in the end, a text prepared by Hosius and Alexander prevailed. They were probably helped by a young deacon, secretary to the bishop of Alexandria, named Athanasius. The resulting text is the so-called Nicene Creed that is repeated to this day, albeit in a slightly expanded form, in all Catholic churches during mass and accepted by nearly all Christian denominations as the expression of their belief. It explicitly states that Christ is *homoousios* or "co-substantial" with God. The term is said to have been proposed by Constantine himself; if so, then probably at the initiative of Hosius, who had previously consulted with Alexander and Athanasius. Its adoption as *the* Creed was tantamount to the condemnation of the doctrine of Arius. This last was confirmed in further articles.

The Council also dealt with the business of Christians who, for various reasons, had separated from the church in recent times. They—especially Melitios and his followers—were treated rather leniently. On the other hand, efforts were made to strengthen the hierarchy by tightening requirements and procedures for the election of bishops. In principle, an election should be conducted by all the bishops of a given ecclesiastical province. Members of the clergy were forbidden to move from town to town. A hierarchy of bishops was established, i.e., provincial bishops were subordinated to metropolitan bishops. This corresponded exactly to the scheme of administrative division of the empire. Finally, special privileges were confirmed for the bishops of Alexandria, Rome, Antioch, and, in part, Jerusalem.

It is worth remembering that the Council of Nicaea also set the date of Easter for the first Sunday after the full moon after the spring equinox. This had been a long-standing practice in the Egyptian and Roman communities, while in many others, the commemoration of the resurrection had been celebrated according to the Jewish calendar. Constantine, not too sympathetic to the Jews, welcomed this resolution.

There was also an interesting provision regarding the marriage of priests. Those who married before ordination did not have to part with their wives. This matter was debated especially vigorously, and the opinion of Bishop Paphnutius of Egypt prevailed. He enjoyed great respect because he had been tortured and mutilated during the persecution. Nevertheless, he was not a fanatic and showed great forbearance and understanding for human frailty. On July 25, the emperor celebrated the twentieth anniversary of his reign. On this occasion, he gave a reception in his palace for the members of the Council. The reception also marked the closing of the first ecumenical council in the history of Christianity.

After the Council

Only two bishops refused to affix their signatures to the act condemning Arius. By order of the emperor, both went into exile—as did Arius himself. A few months later, also by order of the emperor, two other bishops were deposed from their ecclesiastical offices and exiled to remote areas: Eusebius of Nicomedia and Theognis of Nicaea. Both had supported Arianism during the Council; both accepted the Nicene Creed in appearance only; and both continued to oppose its resolutions. The emperor also accused Eusebius of having spied for Licinius during the last war. New bishops were elected to the vacant episcopal sees of Nicaea and Nicomedia—with the approval of the court, of course. All of this clearly showed how, going forward, the secular government intended to intervene in internal Church matters, vigorously assisting certain ecclesiastical factions in their struggle with others.

Yet, Constantine was not opposed to Arianism on doctrinal grounds. In fact, he treated theological problems rather indifferently, and if the surviving texts are to be believed, his own views on the subject were exceptionally vague. The emperor used harsh repression against the opponents of the mainstream Church for purely political reasons. He desired a monolithic unity of the Church, believing that the cohesiveness of its organization and doctrine should correspond to the current political situation when—after so many years of division— there was again only one empire and only one emperor.

From Constantine's point of view, it would have been best if Arius and his followers had voluntarily acknowledged their error and signed on to the Council's resolutions. The emperor did not cease in his efforts to bring this about. He corresponded with Arius. At the same time, many at court, and even in the imperial family, favored the doctrine condemned at Nicaea. Probably as early as the beginning of 327, Arius found himself in Nicomedia. He was summoned before the emperor. As a result of the meeting, he made a declaration, which Constantine considered sufficient proof of submission.

A new convention of bishops, formally constituting a second session of the council, was convened in Nicaea, though it was attended in much smaller numbers. Arius and his followers were received back into the community. It even appears that the final resolutions of the council prudently avoided the contentious term *homoousios*, "co-substantial."

Theognis and Eusebius returned to their former offices, and

the emperor demanded that the bishop of Alexandria also accept Arius as a full member of the clergy in that city. However, to Alexander, who initially agreed with the resolutions of the second council, this last demand was unacceptable. The bishop died in April 328, and a few weeks later, despite a split among the Egyptian clergy, a successor was elected. This was the former deacon Athanasius, the closest associate of the deceased. The emperor very quickly confirmed his election. Too quickly and hastily, as it soon turned out.

However, we have run a little too ahead of ourselves. It is time to go back in time to discuss other events, no less dramatic.

Part Four
CONSTANTINOPLE

The Case of Crispus and Fausta

Constantine opened the twentieth year of his reign with a celebration on July 25, 325, in Nicomedia, just as the First Council of Nicaea was closing its deliberations. Since the celebration was traditionally held in the empire's capital, Rome, the emperor decided to repeat it there. He set out west overland through the Danubian provinces, probably in March 326. He arrived in Aquileia in April, in Milan at the beginning of July, and solemnly entered Rome on the 18th of that month. He had a short stay on the Tiber, less than a month. In September, he returned to Milan, and by the end of the year, we already see him on the eastern side of the Alps, in Sirmium on the Sava.

This was to be Constantine's last visit to Rome. We do not know much about its course, but some echoes allow us to conclude that a disagreement occurred between the emperor and the Senate. Constantine refused to participate in a ceremony during which he was expected to offer a sacrifice at the temple of Jupiter on the Capitol. We should remember that the people of Rome were mostly still followers of ancient deities, which, they believed, had given their city dominion over the world. They felt themselves heirs and guardians of a great tradition. In any case, it is striking that just before leaving the capital, Constantine decided to appoint a new Prefect of Rome. He was a representative of the old aristocracy, a pagan, and since the emperor had appointed prefects from among Christians in the past, this gives the impression that he now saw fit to make some concession in order not to aggravate the conflict. Of course, this sojourn in Rome must have further strengthened Constantine's aversion to that city. Who knows—perhaps it influenced his plan to expand his new residence on the Bosphorus.

But the most important event of 326 was a tragedy in the imperial family. It is difficult today to determine its causes and course or even the chronology of the events. However, the facts themselves are clear, well-attested, and eloquent enough in their raw horror.

First, in the spring or early summer, Constantine put to death his first-born son, the naval hero of the last war with Licinius. Reportedly, the emperor's wife—and the boy's stepmother, Fausta—accused the young man of an attempted rape. Crispus died in Polia, today's Croatian Pula, on the Istrian peninsula.

Soon thereafter, already in Rome, it was Fausta's turn. She was accused of committing adultery. Constantine ordered her locked in an overheated bathhouse, where she suffocated. People said that the emperor's mother, Helena, had been shocked by the death of her first grandson and hell-bent on Fausta's destruction. She believed that Crispus had been innocent and Fausta's accusation was false. She persuaded her son that a crime was best washed away with a crime.

Clearly, relations in the imperial family were not idyllic. It is easy to understand that Fausta hated her stepson, Crispus, because she wanted her sons to inherit the throne. The young man's recent successes only intensified her hatred. To get rid of him, she hatched an intrigue, later exposed by Helena. And we know about Helena that she had ruthlessly persecuted her own stepsons, that is, those his father had with his lawful wife, Theodora. Thanks to her intrigues, the two of them, Dalmatius and Julius Constantius, had to stay away from court for years, in exile in Aquitaine.

But in addition to personal animosities, there may have been other reasons for the drama. In the spring of 326, on his way to Rome, the emperor drafted several laws that severely punished such offenses as adultery, elopement, and the keeping of concubines by married men. The question arises whether these laws were issued in response to Crispus's alleged transgression or whether, conversely, the emperor had to punish his wife and son ruthlessly in order to show personal compliance with his own laws.

One source tells us that Constantine, realizing the monstrosity of what he had done, sought help from pagan priests. These answered him that they did not know of a rite that could cleanse a man of such a crime. A certain Egyptian then appeared at court. He assured the ruler that the Christian religion had the power to take away all sins; from then on, Constantine became an ardent follower of the new faith.[112]

The story is fictional, for the emperor had already cast his lot with Christianity much earlier, but it suggests that circles unfriendly to the ruler tried to exploit the grim case of Crispus and Fausta to discredit his religious policies. Already in antiquity, one heard the opinion that Constantine had stained himself with crimes worthy of Nero. And indeed, when it came to murdering family members, these two were strikingly similar.

Helena in Palestine

Helena lived in Rome for several years in a palace called the Sessorium, near the Lateran. A little outside the city, on the road leading to Praeneste—today's Palestrina—she erected a large tomb for her husband Constantius. The remains of this magnificent octagonal building, in which she herself was later laid to rest, are now known as Tor Pignattara.

Probably at the end of 326, that is, soon after Constantine's departure from Rome, Helena also left the capital. She made the long journey to Palestine to inspect—this was the official purpose—the

---

[112] Zosimos, *Nova Historia*, II 29

construction of churches commanded by her son. Wherever she visited, the empress generously supported the poor and the infirm, and her trip took on the character of a pilgrimage, pious and charitable. We naturally suspect that the real reason for the journey was the recent family tragedy and the desire to blot out her crimes with acts of pious generosity. A curious thing: Constantine himself was in no hurry to visit his Middle Eastern provinces, but he sent his elderly and failing mother most willingly.

Of all the churches in Palestine, the most important was the church erected in Jerusalem over a grotto believed to be the tomb of Christ. A temple of Aphrodite, built under Hadrian, had previously stood on the site. Constantine ordered it demolished and even the earth from under its foundations removed, for he claimed that the whole site had been defiled by demons—this sheds an interesting light on Constantine's religious ideas. The emperor spared no expense to make the church look as magnificent as possible. New orders and instructions kept flowing to Jerusalem. The basilica was finally finished around 335 and called the Church of the Resurrection or the Holy Sepulcher. What its original shape was, we know mainly from descriptions, for over the centuries, it was repeatedly destroyed and rebuilt almost from scratch.

Another church, also very famous, was built over the grotto in Bethlehem, where, according to tradition, Christ had been born. Here, many more fragments remain of the first structure. Finally, a third church was erected on the Mount of Olives, from where Christ was said to have ascended to heaven.

Helena's pilgrimage soon became the source and subject of many legends. Perhaps the most famous is the story of the discovery of the True Cross. Helen was said to have discovered it near the tomb, along with two other crosses. To determine which of them was the sacred cross, she touched each to the body of a bedridden man, and it proved that only one had the power to heal. The empress took a piece of the holy cross to her palace in Rome; as for the nails, she had them melted down and put into her son's helmet. This legend, known in various versions and forms, began to take shape as early as the late fourth century.

On her way back, Helena died in or near Nicomedia. Her son, to honor his mother's memory, gave her name to one of the cities in the province of Bithynia; it was henceforth called Helenopolis. But the body of the empress was taken to Rome and buried in the family mausoleum next to the body of Constantius. The great hall of her palace of Sessorium was turned into a church. This basilica, rebuilt in the 18th century, is now called Santa Croce in Gerusalemme. This is not the only church in Rome dating back to the time of Constantine; there are several, two of which are very famous.

The Basilicas of Rome

The palace of the Lateranus family was located on the hill of Celius in Rome. After Constantine's victory over Maxentius, it passed into the possession of Empress Fausta. The episcopal commission, which heard the Donatist case in 313, sat within its walls. Probably already by that time, a house chapel existed within the precincts of the palace. In later years, a great church was built here financed by the emperor, the first within the city walls and the seat of the bishops of Rome. As a papal cathedral, it still bears the proud title of "Mother and Head of all the churches of the city and the world." Until the beginning of the tenth century, it was called the Basilica of the Savior, but later, after a major restoration, it was given a new patron saint—Saint John the Baptist.

The Lateran church was not built in imitation of pagan temples. The builders consciously broke with the old model to emphasize the distinctiveness of the new religion. Besides, Christian tabernacles had a different function, as they had to accommodate large crowds of believers during services. They were built on the plan of large Roman secular buildings called basilicas. Roman basilicas had been ornate halls where court hearings and public ceremonies were held. They were rectangular buildings with flat roofs and were divided into lengthwise naves by rows of columns. In the Lateran basilica, the wide central nave had two parallel naves on each side.

The Lateran church introduced several new architectonic features that would eventually be part of most later Christian basilicas. In addition to the central, elongated hall, it had another, smaller and narrower, running perpendicular to the long hall about 2/3s of the way down and giving the structure the overall plan of the cross. The altar was located in the transverse section, behind which, in a small apse—a space covered with a semi-circular dome—stood the bishop's throne. Like this:

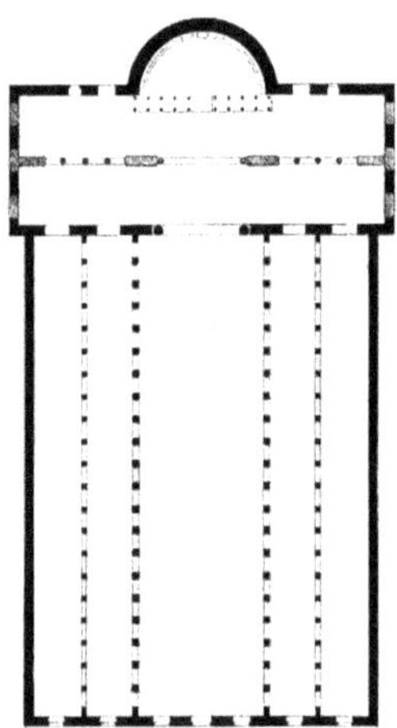

After two major fires in the 14th century, the church was completely rebuilt in the 17th and 18th centuries, and almost nothing has survived since the time of Constantine. Next to the basilica is an octagonal baptistery, or a chapel, where baptismal rites were performed. This building also owes its foundation to the emperor, but its present shape comes from slightly later times, from the beginning of the fifth century.

From antiquity until 1309, that is, until the time of the "Avignon captivity," the popes resided in a palace next to the basilica; it was called the "Patriarchium." That palace was demolished at the end of the 14th century, and a new one was erected in its place in the 16th century. It now serves as a museum of ancient Christian art.

Fate dealt just as harshly with the other great basilica built in Rome on the orders of Constantine. This was St. Peter's, erected in the Vatican over the place where—according to tradition—the apostle's body had been buried. That magnificent building accumulated various art treasures over the centuries: mosaics, paintings, bas-reliefs, tombs, and inscriptions. All this was mercilessly demolished at the beginning of the 16th century, during the pontificate of Julius II, to make way for the present basilica, enormous but artistically certainly not the most outstanding. Only recent excavations have told us what the old one had looked like. The same excavations uncovered Roman tombs from the time of the construction of Constantine's Basilica. One of the very few relics of the first temple is a large bronze cone: the faithful washed their hands with the water flowing from its scales.

Legend has it that the emperor himself initiated the construction of the basilica on his first or second stay in Rome; however, it seems much more likely that the church owes its creation to the events of the year 326.

Probably at the same time, the walls of the third basilica began to go up on the road to Ostia over the tomb of Apostle Paul. It was rebuilt at the end of the fourth century and survived in its original state without any major changes until 1828 when it was consumed by fire. The structure of the present church corresponds faithfully to the plan of the old one.

The City of Constantine

But Constantine's most feverish construction activity took place not in Palestine and not in Rome but in the city on the Bosphorus, which had hitherto been called Byzantion, or Byzantium.

Constantine disliked Rome and never stayed there for more than two or three months. But when he united the Empire under his rule, he was faced, as Diocletian once was, with the question of where to establish his headquarters. Only the Balkan or Asia Minor provinces were an option, for they were the geographical center of the vast state, and the most important strategic and trade routes ran through them. From here, it was easiest to watch over the security of the Danubian and Eastern borders, which were then the most threatened. The emperor would probably have been glad to settle in Sirmium or Serdica, but both of these cities lay deep inland. Nicomedia had some advantages, but it had unpleasant associations with Diocletian, Galerius, and Licinius. It is said that Constantine was even thinking of expanding Ilion, or ancient Troy, where, according to legend, the ancestors of the Romans had come from, but Ilion had no natural harbor. In the end, the choice fell on Byzantium, which met all the requirements set by the emperor.

The city lay on a hilly peninsula at the entrance to the Bosphorus Strait, between the Propontis, or Sea of Marmara, and the narrow inlet of Golden Horn. Already in classical times, it played a significant role as a point where land and sea routes crossed. Constantine must have taken note of the city's strategic location during the war of 324 when it so successfully repelled his siege. Probably still that year, immediately after Licinius's surrender, he gave it a new name: Constantinopolis, or the City of Constantine. However, this did not yet mean that the emperor planned to establish his residence there. A dozen years earlier, he had ordered the rebuilding of Cirta, the most prominent city in Numidia, and gave it the name Constantina, a name which it still bears today (Constantine/Kasantina, Algeria); yet the ruler never honored the city even with the briefest visit.

It seems that the decision to make Constantinople his permanent seat was not made until 326, after the unfortunate events in Rome, which intensified the emperor's aversion to the imperial capital. From then on, work began on a grand scale. The new city was solemnly inaugurated on May 11, 330. This date was to be celebrated annually for over a millennium as Constantinople's birthday, analogous to April 21 in Rome. It is characteristic that pagan rituals were preserved during the inauguration; even an astrologer's advice was sought when choosing the auspicious day. The celebrations lasted for forty days. Sacrifices were made to the gods, and in the circus, before the chariot races began, a statue of the emperor was carried around the stadium. It was made of wood and gilded, and in its right hand, it held a statuette of the goddess Tyche—the Lady of the City's Fate. Taking his seat in the imperial box on that occasion, Constantine is said to have made his first appearance wearing a diadem. This ornament became part of the Imperial regalia from then on—it is the ancestor of our crown. In addition to traditional ceremonies in honor of ancient deities, there were also Christian services.

An effort was made to preserve as much as possible of the old Byzantium, but, in truth, a completely new city was being created all around it: giving it a new name was not just a formality. The emperor quadrupled its area, moving far to the west its defensive wall that ran across the peninsula, from the Sea of Marmara to the Bay of the Golden Horn. He also spared no expense to grace his capital with a multitude of magnificent buildings. Like old Rome, the city was divided into fourteen administrative districts. Constantinople was to have its Capitol, its Curia, or the Senate meeting hall, its Forum, and even its Via Sacra. The imperial palaces were arranged among parks and gardens that terraced down to the Sea of Marmara. Other public buildings clustered around a square called the Augusteum and about the aforementioned Forum. As in any great city, circuses, baths, and basilicas were erected. To decorate them, various provinces were ruthlessly stripped of their works of art. Columns, statues, and bas-reliefs were brought from everywhere. Even the temple at Delphi had to donate: it gave up a huge bronze tripod, the votive gift commemorating the Greeks' victory over the Persians more than eight hundred years earlier.

It is noteworthy that in the course of expanding the city, previously existing pagan temples were respected. Thus, for example, the sanctuary of the Dioscuri was integrated into the city plan. Moreover, two new pagan temples were built: of the goddess Tyche and of the goddess Rhea. A great porphyry column was set up in the Forum, and on it—a statue of Constantine. It was cast in bronze, and a radiant crown made the ruler resemble the Sun God. In contrast, the two Christian basilicas near the Augusteum were given names that were not so much religious as philosophical: Sophia, or Wisdom, and Eirene, or Peace. The first of these, completely rebuilt by Emperor Justinian, is the famous Hagia Sophia.

At the edge of the city stood the Church of the Holy Apostles, and next to it, a mausoleum where the remains of the emperor and the members of his family were to rest.

In order to speed up the construction of the city and ease the burden to the treasury, the emperor introduced many administrative and economic benefits for those who settled here and built houses. Consequently, the number of residents grew rapidly. They were mostly Greeks from neighboring provinces; indeed, despite the emperor's best efforts, only a few families of the old Roman aristocracy decided to move from Rome to Constantinople. As a result, contrary to the ruler's hopes, the use of Latin was, from the very beginning, limited to the narrow court and military circles.

The city was granted certain privileges previously enjoyed only by the capital of the Empire; first of all, its territory was exempted from taxes and tributes. Grain was distributed among its residents at greatly reduced prices. The city council was given the title of Senate. (It ranked lower than the Roman Senate and this was manifested in the titles of the Senators: the Senators from the Tiberian capital were called *clarissimi* while those from the Bosphorus were only called *clari*). The city was governed by a governor with the title of proconsul; only after 359 was Constantinople headed by a *Praefectus urbi*, like Rome.

Even these minor facts—small but very telling—prove that Constantine did not think of moving the capital to his new seat. Formally, the ancient Latin city, the cradle of the Empire, remained the capital. However, the permanent residence of the ruler had to become the *de facto* center of the state. Gradually, and only after the reign of Constantine, did this come to be reflected in formal legal acts.

It seems highly unlikely that the term "New Rome" or "Second Rome" was used in the days of Constantine. It appears in literature and legal records much later—only in the fifth century. On the other hand, the inhabitants themselves have always proudly called themselves Romans.[113]

Constantine and Athanasius

And so, Constantine now resided in his new magnificent seat, ruling the vast Empire all by himself. It seemed that everyone had to bow to his will. And yet, there were matters against which even his imperial majesty proved powerless.

In 328, Athanasius became bishop of Alexandria: a man still young at the time, less than thirty, but widely known since the Council of Nicaea, when he distinguished himself as a deacon-counselor to Alexander and one of Arius' fiercest opponents. A Hellenized Egyptian, he spoke Greek and Coptic. Like all fanatics, he was stubborn and tenacious, and his intellectual horizons were limited. He had an unshakeable conviction that only he was on the right path, and whoever dared to have a different opinion had to be destroyed. In his personal life, his conduct was saintly, but to achieve his goals, he was prepared to resort to any means necessary.

Athanasius rejected the demand to restore Arius to ecclesiastical dignity in Alexandria even more forcefully than his predecessor had done. Such an attitude on the part of the bishop must have led to conflict, especially since the pro-Arian party seemed to be taking the upper hand in Constantine's entourage. This included above all, the emperor's half-sister, Constance, and the bishop of Nicomedia, Eusebius. After Helena's death, Constantine's half-brother, Julius Constantius, arrived from Gaul and soon married a close relative of Eusebius, Basilina. From their marriage, Julian, the later emperor, called the Apostate, was born.

Athanasius had against him not only Arians but also Melitians, still very numerous in Egypt. The latter accused the bishop

---

[113] Re the founding of Constantinople: R. Janin, *Constantinople Byzantine,* Paris 1950, p. 27-37

of accepting for church use linen which should have been handed over to the state. Athanasius was summoned to Nicomedia. Here, he suffered a new setback, for he had sent a coffer of gold to a certain high dignitary, who meanwhile fell into disfavor. Nevertheless, he obtained an audience with the emperor and managed to clear himself of all charges. In 332, he was back in his homeland.

But already the following year, a new conflict broke out, now caused by Athanasius, who tried to bring the Mareotis district south of Alexandria under his jurisdiction. A priest sent by him acted violently. He overturned the altar in one of the churches, smashed the sacrificial chalice, and burned the liturgical books used during service. The Melitians now came forward with the accusation that Athanasius had murdered one of their priests, embalmed his hand, and was using it to perform witchcraft. This was, of course, completely made up, and the alleged murder victim was soon found enjoying robust health and free use of both his hands, but the bad odor of witchcraft clung to Athanasius for a long time.

Faced with the mounting conflict, Constantine convened a synod of bishops. It was first held in Palestinian Caesarea in 334, but Athanasius did not show up. He claimed that all those attending it were his enemies. He did, however, appear at the second session of this synod in the Phoenician city of Tyre. The emperor sent his observers there. Athanasius's opponents—not only Arians—presented a long list of charges against him, both real and fabricated. A commission was sent to Egypt to investigate the validity of the charges on the spot, and the synod moved to Jerusalem. There, in September of 334, the Basilica of the Holy Sepulcher was consecrated, and the commission produced its report. On the basis of it, Athanasius was found guilty and removed from the episcopal office.

Seeing no other hope, Athanasius went to Constantinople. He behaved humbly and asked only that a new commission be summoned, this time in the presence of the emperor. The latter, apparently moved by the attitude of the supplicant, agreed and summoned the bishops from Jerusalem to the capital. Before they arrived, however, a new accusation against Athanasius emerged: he was said to have attempted to interfere with grain shipments from Egypt to Constantinople. The accusation had to have come with some evidence, for the emperor reacted quickly and harshly: Athanasius was exiled far to the west, all the way to Trier in Gaul. He returned from the rainy north only after Constantine's death. And soon rekindled old quarrels.

After the exile of Athanasius, Arius was finally able to return to Alexandria. However, he soon found himself on the Bosphorus again. For as soon as he set foot on Egyptian soil, riots broke out between his supporters and his enemies. Arius died soon after his arrival in Constantinople. Death took him suddenly. Athanasius even exploited his death for propaganda purposes; he claimed that Arius had died in a latrine.[114]

Temples and Finance

Were it only the Athanasius affair that plagued the Christian communities and troubled the emperor! Soon, there were other flashpoints as well. In Syrian Antioch, a dangerous dispute broke out soon after 330 over the staffing of the bishop's curia. In Africa, meanwhile, the Donatists were just as powerful as before. Around 330, they seized a large new church in Numidian Cirta—that Constantina rebuilt by order of the emperor. Constantine hurled abominations against the Donatists, but only in letters. He left revenge to the Heavens for the time being and ordered a new temple to be built for the Orthodox Catholics in Cirta. Thus, Christianity, which was supposed to provide ideological and organizational support for the unity of the empire, caused a host of intractable difficulties instead. To deal with its internal conflicts, which had lain hidden during the period of persecution, Christians increasingly sought help from the secular authority.

---

[114] Re Athanasius see E. Schwartz, *Gesamte Schriften*, III, Berlin 1959

Meanwhile, the state struggled with serious difficulties of yet another nature: financial and economic. They involved, as one can easily guess, the enormous cost of building Constantinople and heavy military expenditures. The emperor had always been generous to his soldiers, as even his enemies admitted. But now, in order to meet his enormous expenses, he liquidated the large reserves accumulated by the frugal Licinius. Even that did not last long: it seems that at one point, some mints ran out of bullion and suspended all activity. It was necessary to find new sources of revenue.

Compelled by hard necessity, Constantine used methods already practiced by some Roman emperors before him, though probably never on such a scale. He confiscated precious objects of gold, silver, bronze, and copper which had collected over the centuries in the temples of various deities; even some cult statues seem to have been melted down. It seems that the landed estates of some temples were also seized for the benefit of the imperial treasury, at least in some provinces. These seizures were sometimes carried out very brutally. Christian communities, of course, seized the opportunity to mock pagan cults and show the powerlessness of their "demons." However, with very few exceptions, the temples themselves remained open, and sacrifices continued. The claim made by some Christian sources that Constantine closed all temples and banned sacrifices is not true. The learned Libanius of Syrian Antioch, remembering those days, said: "The temples were poor, but all the ceremonies of worship were performed."

We should note that Constantine remained the high priest of the old Roman religion until the end of his days, for he never relinquished the title of *Pontifex Maximus*. He also consented to the establishment of priestly colleges in various lands for the worship of the imperial family (*sacerdotium gentis Flaviae*). Already in the last years of his reign, he allowed a temple of the Flavian Family to be built in the town of Hispellum in Italian Umbria;[115] he only stipulated that it not be marred by "some contagious superstition," that is, the

---

[115] Modern Spello

worship of a pagan deity other than his family. The town itself was given the name of "Flavia Constans." It follows that he treated the worship of his family as a kind of official state religion—secular in its essence, but nevertheless a religion.[116]

The seizure of temple estates yielded significant profits but was a one-time deal. More important was the expansion of the tax system. Constantine maintained the tribute system introduced by Diocletian, that is, the *iugatio* and the *capitatio*. However, those taxes were paid in kind, and the treasury needed bullion. Therefore, even before the first conflict with Licinius, Constantine began to impose taxes payable in coin. One, called *follis senatorius*, burdened the estates of the landed aristocracy. Another, *collatio lustralis*, affected merchants and artisans in the cities, and even—prostitutes; it was payable in gold or silver every five years.

Hand in hand with the expansion of the tax system went other reforms of the tax apparatus. It was headed by two high dignitaries— ministers, we would say today. One bore the title *comes sacrarum largitionum* and administered the "sacred generosity" (the state treasury), while the other, *comes rei privatae*, was in charge of the emperor's private estates.

An important goal of all these efforts was to simplify the monetary system. In part, it succeeded. The gold coin, the so-called *solidus*, retained the weight that Constantine had given it sometime before 312: 1/72 of a Roman pound, or 4.4 grains. The same was true of the silver coin, called the *siliqua*, which weighed 1/144 of a pound. On the other hand, copper and silver-plated coins were minted in insufficient quantities, which caused some market distortions.

Wars, Army, Veterans

Military spending must have been the biggest line item in the state

---

[116] Libanius, Speeches, 30, 6. Hispellum: H. Dessau, *Inscriptiones Latinae Selectae*, no. 705

budget, certainly larger than the cost of building Constantinople. Despite the unification of the empire, a large army was still necessary due to the constant threat to the borders. The situation on the Danube and the Rhine was the worst. Over the security of the former, the emperor kept personal vigil. In 328, he crossed the Danube several times and defeated both Sarmatians and Goths. In that year, his son Constantine II, then residing in Trier, vanquished the Alemanni. Recalled later to the Danubian provinces, he inflicted a terrible defeat on the Goths in the winter 331/332. Surrounded by the Romans, great masses of barbarians died of hunger and cold. The remainder sued for peace and, for a time, became Roman allies, defending the borders of the Empire and providing auxiliary contingents. In return, the Emperor sent food supplies across the Danube.

In 334, Constantine stood on the middle Danube again because a civil war broke out among the Sarmatians in the present-day Hungary. A part of this people, driven from their homes by a revolt of the lower classes, sought refuge within the borders of the Empire. It is said that nearly three hundred thousand people were accepted as refugees and settled in various provinces, from the Danube to Gaul.

The eastern, Persian border, on the other hand, was at first quiet. Alas, after a while, things began to escalate there as well, and in 337, a great war threatened to break out.

It is difficult to say to what extent the military reform of the period, which had taken a long time to implement, dates back to the time of Diocletian and to what extent it is the work of Constantine. However, it seems that the contribution of the latter was very important and perhaps even decisive. It was he who completed the division of the army into *limitanei,* or frontier troops, and *comitatenses,* or combat troops, stationed somewhat inland. Under Diocletian, the latter category was just taking shape and was still very limited in number. From the time of Constantine also derived a clear division of the *comitatenses* into two types of arms, under separate commands: infantry under *magister peditum,* and cavalry under *magister equitum.* The number of legions significantly increased, but from now on, they were relatively small, having, on average, about a thousand men each, and that only foot. (The cavalry formations were called *vexillationes*).

In place of the praetorian cohorts, abolished in 312, the emperor introduced the so-called *scholae palatinae*. These were cavalry units of one thousand (later five hundred) men each, selected mostly from Germanic warriors. In general, Constantine took barbarians into service willingly and *en masse*. The auxiliary troops, or *auxilia*, in the frontier armies were largely composed of them. Constantine's successors continued this method of replenishing the armed forces. Barely Romanized Germanic officers sometimes reached the highest offices, while the army gradually became a foreign body. This was to have disastrous political consequences.

If the emperor was forced to resort to such a method of recruitment (in which he was certainly not the first), it was mainly because the inhabitants of the empire were evading military service. Cases of self-inflicted injuries (such as cutting off fingers) were so frequent that the emperor had to devote a separate law to the matter.[117] And yet, a soldier's life was not bad: he was well-paid, and after twenty or so years of service, he received tax exemptions for himself and his family. Constantine also allowed his soldiers to occupy uncultivated land on favorable terms, for such land was to be forever free of all tribute, while the settlers received a certain amount of money for the purchase of farm implements, as well as a couple of oxen and a hundred measures of various seeds. A veteran who preferred to devote himself to trade was subject to taxes only if his capital exceeded the limit of one hundred thousand *folles*.[118]

Those leaving the service knew how to assert their rights. This is shown particularly vividly in the preface to a certain edict of Constantine. It is an excerpt from the minutes of a meeting between the emperor and discharged veterans. The event probably took place in March 320:

"When the emperor entered the main quarters, he was greeted by

---

[117] C. Th. VII 22, 1
[118] C. Th. VII 20, 3

prefects, tribunes, and officers of higher ranks with the cry:

"Constantine Augustus, may the gods preserve thee for us! Your health is our health! We speak the truth! We speak under oath!"

But the assembled veterans jeered:

"Constantine Augustus, why do you dismiss us from service without our promised relief?"

Constantine Augustus said:

"I should not reduce but multiply the benefits of my fellow veterans!"

Veteran Victorinus said sarcastically:

"May your benefits not crush us with their astonishing weight!"

Constantine Augustus demanded:

"Say openly what ails you!"

All the veterans said:

"You can see for yourself!"

The emperor then spoke, enumerating a number of privileges which he had already bestowed on his veterans. They are not subject to any civilian obligations and may not be drafted for corvee; nor may any fees or tributes be collected from them.[119]

The Changing Shape of the Roman Society

The aforementioned law stipulated that the sons of veterans who cut off their fingers to avoid military service were to be treated the same as *curiales*, bearing all the burdens and duties of the state. But who were these *curiales*?

Their history is both paradoxical and significant. In the early days of the empire, being a member of this social class was an object of

---

[119] C. Th. VII 20, 2

pride and of strenuous pursuit by the wealthy.

Curiales (also called *decuriones*) had once been members of municipal councils. They decided local matters, enjoyed great authority, and represented their cities before the provincial governor and even the emperor. They held their dignity for life. Admittedly, *curiales* were also responsible for law and order in the city and for the fulfillment of obligations imposed by the state. However, in the centuries of general prosperity, peace and rule of law, this responsibility did not pose special problems. The situation changed completely during the third century, a period of unending wars and upheavals. The state crushed the cities with more and more burdens, and the *curiales*, who vouched for their cities personally with all their wealth, soon became a caste of hereditary tax collectors. Of course, in this new state of affairs, decuriones would have been glad to relinquish their troublesome dignity. However, there was no way to do it because the state considered this honorable function not only lifelong but also hereditary.

Constantine devoted a great deal of attention to the curial class from the beginning of his reign. Quite a number of his decrees on the subject have been preserved. Their general drift is to tighten state controls over this dignified but embittered class. Its position at the time is most clearly illuminated by the fact that many *curiales* volunteered for the army. They preferred the hard discipline of the camp and the dangers of war to the constant harassment of tax authorities. The phenomenon had to be widespread, since in 335 the emperor ordered that all *curiales* be expelled from the ranks of the army. They were to return to their former cities and resume their former duties.[120]

And yet we have seen that the army had trouble enlisting recruits. And it had to be serious trouble because the same Constantine insisted that the sons of a veteran should also serve as soldiers. Nevertheless, in the case of *curiales*, the emperor gave priority to the economic needs of the state over its defense.

---

[120] C. Th. XII 1, 22

Equally significant is an earlier decree, also from 326, concerning those *curiales* who had joined the ranks of the Christian clergy in order to escape their obligations (since all priests were exempt from all duties). Accordingly, the emperor decreed that a vacant ecclesiastical office can only be assumed by a person who does not belong to a curial family or whose wealth is so small that it does not obligate him to stand surety for his city. For, as the emperor stated in his concluding sentence, rich people must shoulder the burden of the state for the sake of the general good, while the poor should benefit from the wealth of the church.[121] A dozen years after Constantine's death, the same rule was applied to the sons of priests as to the sons of veterans: if they did not take up their fathers' profession, they should be treated as *curiales*.[122]

Not only soldiers and *curiales* inherited their professions. The same process was also taking place in other professions, especially in those that were crucial to economic life. This was caused by a widespread labor shortage and the return to an economy based largely on contributions in labor. This made the state anxious to preserve the human resources of every profession. The process had been going on for a long time and was steadily gaining momentum as the overall economic situation deteriorated. Constantine's reign was only one stage in this transition, inevitably moving the society towards the feudal order, but the period of his rule was key: very many laws of Constantine established or mandated succession of professions. These included bakers and the so-called *navicularii*, i.e., owners of properties to which the duty to build and equip a naval ship was attached. (Admittedly, in return, these *navicularii* were exempt from all other burdens, tributes, and labor).[123]

Another law stipulated that the sons of officials should also serve as officials.[124] As is common in all bureaucracies, the

---

[121] C. Th. XVI 2, 6
[122] C. Th. XVI 2, 9
[123] C. Th. XIII 5, 2
[124] C. Th. VII, 22, 3

administration—the mainstay and foundation of the system—was poorly remunerated and treated negligently; therefore, the more capable and energetic individuals sought to escape from the profession of a scribe. We should note, however, that we may also interpret this law in a different way: as a privilege, guaranteeing the inheritance of positions, admittedly poorly paid, but secure and, thanks to bribery and abuse, providing ample opportunity for "side" earnings.

Extremely important, even historic, is the law of October 30, 332:

> The lord in whose estate a fugitive *colonus* is found must not only return him, but also pay tax [*capitatio*] for the entire period during which the said *colonus* stayed with him. In cases of suspicion that the *colonus* intends to escape again, he can be shackled like a slave.[125]

A *colonus* was a personally free tenant farmer of a plot of land on a large estate. In some provinces of the Empire, such *coloni* had been "attached to the land" before (that is, not free to change their place of residence or type of work), and during the third century, this phenomenon spread very widely. However, it is only since the issuance of Constantine's laws that it can be called *glebae adscriptio*, or "attribution to the land." And thus, an important pillar of feudalism—serfdom—becomes a binding legal norm with this emperor.

Teachers, Doctors, Architects

The above clearly shows that the emperor managed rights and obligations of even those classes and estates that he highly valued and cared for. This was the case with the clergy and the veterans. But he also gave special favors to certain professions of the *intelligentsia*. Continuing the policies of some of his predecessors, he issued several important laws in this spirit.

---

[125] C. Th. V 17, 1

The first of these, published in 321, contained the following provisions:

> Doctors, teachers, and professors are exempted from all duties; this applies both to the persons themselves and to the property in their possession in their cities of residence. Whoever harms such persons shall pay a hundred thousand to the treasury as a penalty. If the damage is done by a slave, he is to be lashed with a whip by his master in front of the wronged party; alternatively, the master may pay twenty thousand to the treasury, while the slave is to be retained as a pledge until the sum is paid in full. Doctors, teachers, and professors must be paid their outstanding salaries and fees. If they wish, they may hold municipal dignities; however, it is forbidden to force them to do so.[126]

Five years later, in 326, a law was published exempting the palace and city physicians (*archiatri*) from all obligations to the state and even extending this privilege to their sons.[127]

Seven years later, in 333, Constantine confirmed all the decrees of previous emperors granting doctors, teachers, and professors an exemption from state burdens and extended this relief to their wives and sons as well. He also decreed that the aforementioned were not subject to compulsory military service and that their homes were not to be used to quarter soldiers. The concluding sentence, explaining the grounds for this imperial favor, is very telling:

> So that they can more easily train as many people as possible in the liberal sciences and in other skills.[128]

Constantine took great care to develop a cadre of educated people. He wrote of this openly in a letter to the governor of Africa in the year 324:

> Very many architects are needed, but there are none. Therefore, may Your Excellence urge this study to those people in the African provinces who, being about twenty years old, have already passed

---

[126]C. Th. XIII 3, 1
[127] C. Th. XIII 3, 2
[128] C. Th. XIII 3, 3

the course of the liberal sciences. In order to make it easier for them, we exempt them and their parents from the burden of corvee; and they should also be paid while they are studying.[129]

Thus, Emperor Constantine deserves to be remembered by all those today who feel they are the heirs of the doctors, architects, teachers and professors of sixteen centuries ago.

New Offices

The stipulation that the sons of clerks were to take up their fathers' profession becomes fully understandable if one considers the great multiplication of all sorts of offices under Constantine. Each one employed multitudes of registrars, notaries, scribes, and accountants. In this respect, the emperor's activities were indeed groundbreaking and were a precursor of the Byzantine bureaucratic system.

A detailed account of the organization of the offices would require an extensive study, and we will not attempt it here. And we should remember that during the emperor's lifetime, these *officia* underwent constant transformations, and many important issues concerning their competencies are still being researched. It is also not always clear which reforms were introduced by Constantine and which by his successors. But even a very sketchy picture will allow us to see how vast and complex the machinery of these institutions became under Constantine.

The emperor abolished the system of tetrarchy. Yet, very soon—even before the final showdown with Licinius—he realized that he could not handle the burden of government alone. Gradually, therefore, he developed a new concept for the administration of the empire: he created "Prefectures." While Constantine dissolved the Praetorian cohorts about 312, the high office of their commander remained. It remained because the *Praefectus Praetorio* concentrated

---

[129] C. Th. XIII4, 1

many important functions in his hand and was traditionally regarded as the emperor's closest collaborator. But, unlike his predecessors, Constantine appointed several *Praefecti* simultaneously. By the end of his reign, there were probably five: three in the West and two in the East.

They had very extensive powers, indeed, were somewhat akin to viceroys. This was manifested, for example, in the fact that a prefect's decision could not be appealed to the emperor. The prefects stood over to the vicars of dioceses and the governors of provinces; the latter could no longer contact the sovereign directly. On the other hand, the prefects did not have an armed force at their disposal—although they supplied the troops stationed in their prefectures and paid their salaries. This was in line with a principle consistently applied by Constantine that civilian power had to be separated from military power.

The ultimate government of the empire was the so-called *sacrum consistorium* composed of its highest officials—a kind of cabinet of ministers. Its name came from the fact that its members stood in the presence of the emperor (the Latin *consistere* means "to stand")—for however long the conference lasted. Of course, formally, it was all about showing respect to the emperor. But the custom seems to have made a lot of sense, as it certainly encouraged brevity and matter-of-factness of speeches. Who knows whether the empire would not have fallen sooner if a sitting system had been adopted.

The highest dignitaries of the state enjoyed the title *comes* or "companion"—it still survives today in some languages, for example, the French *comte* or English "count." Constantine bestowed these titles so generously that it soon became necessary to introduce a hierarchy. The *comites* were divided into three categories; only those of the first rank attended the consistory.

One of the most important officials in the ruler's entourage was the *quaestor sacri palatii*. Among his responsibilities was preparing the text of edicts and responding to petitions. *Magister officiorum* headed the chancellery, which had several departments called *scrinia*. He supervised the personal security of the emperor, and the *scholae palatinae*—the mounted imperial guard—reported to him. He supervised court ceremonies. Finally, he liaisoned with the Praetorium Prefects by means of an office called *schola agentium in rebus*. These *agentes*, or agents, had multiple tasks; they were sent on important missions as couriers but also as organs of secret surveillance since the emperor did not trust his clerical apparatus, especially in the provinces. Reports of appalling bribery came constantly, and the enraged ruler threatened to have the stealing hands of bureaucrats chopped off. Prefects were also subject to control by officials from the *schola notariorum*. Their chief, the *primicerius notariorum*, reported directly to the emperor. In principle, however, this *schola* served as the consistory's secretariat, and its main tasks included issuing appointments of officers and clerks.

The palace and services directly related to the person of the ruler, though they exerted great influence on all current affairs, were a world unto themselves. *Praepositus sancti cubiculi*, or the Overseer of the Sacred Bedroom, generally a eunuch, was one of the most influential people in the state. He oversaw a multitude of officials who watched over the emperor's chambers and robes, as well as order and silence during audiences. The higher-ranking members of these services were freedmen, while the lower-ranking were slaves.

Death of Constantine

It was not given to the emperor to spend the last years of his eventful life in peace and serenity. It is true that after 330, he rarely and only briefly left his residence in Constantinople, but he remained there mainly to keep a close watch on the ominous developments in the East.

In 333, riots caused by food shortages due to a major crop failure broke out in the Syrian provinces, especially in Antioch. The following year, one of the high officials in Cyprus proclaimed himself emperor; he was captured and executed. At the same time, relations between the Empire and Persia became increasingly strained. The emperor reportedly resented the Persians' persecution of Christians, while the Persians, for their part, regarded the religion's followers as spies and supporters of Rome—just as Diocletian had once suspected the Manichaeans of favoring the Persians. The fundamental cause of the conflict between the two powers was, of course, the same as ever: a dispute over the borderlands.

It was now necessary to prepare for war. To this end, as early as 333, the emperor installed his middle son, Constantius, in Antioch (he was to ensure that there was no repeat of the recent unrest), and his nephew, Hannibalian, in eastern Asia Minor. And here is an interesting tidbit: Hannibalian was given the title of King of Kings, which had been traditionally used by Persian rulers. This meant in effect that the Empire was claiming dominion over the entire East. The Persians had to respond to this challenge. In early 337, they declared war.

Constantius's assignment to Antioch was also connected with plans to divide the empire in the future. Constantine intended to give the western provinces—Britain, Gaul, and Spain—to his eldest son, Constantine II. Constantius, on the other hand, would rule Egypt, Syria, and Asia Minor, while the youngest Constans would rule the center strip: Italy, Africa, and Pannonia. Nor did Constantine forget his nephews, or rather, strictly speaking, the sons of his half-brother Dalmatius: one of them, Hannibalian, would rule parts of Asia Minor, while the other, Dalmatius, would rule Thrace and Macedonia.

The expected war with Persia did not take place, and negotiations began in the early spring of 337. At the beginning of April, the emperor felt ill. He left for a water cure in a nearby city, then went to Helenopolis to pray at the miraculous relics of the martyr Lucian. He then moved to Nicomedia and settled in its suburbs. He conferred with the bishop of that city, Eusebius. He was baptized by him—an ardent supporter of Arianism! He shed the purple and clothed himself in white robes, indicating that henceforth, he would live only for the matters of the spirit.

This is how the last days of Constantine are depicted in the *Life* attributed to Eusebius of Caesarea. A certain document has been preserved that does not quite square with this tale. It is an edict that came out of the emperor's chancellery on May 21, 337, that is, already after the emperor's baptism. It released the priests of the cult of the ruling family from all state obligations to the state. The text of the decree was engraved on bronze tablets and displayed publicly. It seems that to his last day, the emperor supported those aspects of the old religion that suited him politically.[130]

Constantine died at noon on May 22, 337. His embalmed body was taken to Constantinople, where the highest dignitaries performed an act of adoration before it. The solemn funeral did not take place until Constantius arrived from Antioch. The body was carried in solemn procession from the palace to the Church of the Holy Apostles and laid in a porphyry sarcophagus in the center between twelve empty tombs representing the twelve disciples of Christ. In his vision, Constantine was the thirteenth and the most important.[131]

As a reward for his services to the Church, soon after his death, Christians gave the emperor the nickname "Great." On the other hand, the enemies of the new religion judged the deceased harshly, accusing him of destroying the old order. Even a close relative, the later Emperor Julian, said so repeatedly and publicly. However, with the passage of time, our perspective changes, and with it our evaluation of many things. We are unable to determine today when and to what extent Constantine became a sincere follower of Christianity. On the other hand, we are able to show that political reasons played a large role in his adherence to the church. The emperor thought that the ecclesiastical organization could be useful in his struggle for power and in strengthening the unity of the state. But once he took certain steps in this direction, he became a prisoner of his own decisions, since irreversible facts had occurred.

He significantly reformed the old system of government and wished to give a new shape to many areas of social life: legislation and

---

[130] C. Th. XII 5, 2
[131] *The Life of Constantine* IV 61-75

the economy, the military and the administration. There was certainly a lot of ambition in this, perhaps often excessive ambition. But there was also a sincere concern for ensuring the permanence of the Empire and the welfare of the lower classes, which Constantine had sought to protect from the abuse of the rich and of the corrupt bureaucracy. Above all, what shines through in many of Constantine's works is an intuitive understanding of the direction of the historical changes of the time: an understanding that is always an essential characteristic of any greatness.

In one area, however, Constantine made a huge mistake, although one understandable for many reasons: instead of the co-rulership by choice introduced by Diocletian, he tried to establish a co-rulership by blood. And practically at the emperor's grave, the first act of a new drama began: the falling out among his sons.

THE END

Abbreviations in the Footnotes

C. Th.: *Codex Theodosianus* (The Codex of Theodosius)
Eusebius: Eusebios, *Ekklesiastike Historia* (Eusebius, "The History of the Church")
Eutropius: *Eutropius, Breviarium ab urbe condita* (Eutropius, "A brief history from the founding of the city").
Lactantius: *Lactantius, De mortibus persecutorum* (Lactantius, "On the deaths of persecutors").
The Life of Constantine:*Eis ton Mon tou Makariou Konstantinou Basileos* ("Life of the Blessed Emperor Constantine," a work attributed to Eusebius).

Bibliography

The extant literature on the topic of late Roman Empire is vast. Here are some of the more prominent works:

O. Seeck, *Geschichte des Untergangs der antiken Welt*, I-IV, Berlin 1921;
M. Besnier, *L'Empire Romain de l'evenement de Severes au concile de Nicee*, Paris 1937;
A. Piganiol, *L'Empire Chretien (325-395)*, Paris 1947; this work and the previous one appeared as part of *Histoire Generale*, published by G. Glotz;
E. Stein, *Histoire du Bas-Empire, edition francaise* par. J. R. Palanque, Paris 1949-1959.
The Cambridge Ancient History, vol. XII: The Imperial Crisis and Recovery, Cambridge 1939 (collective);
A. H. M. Jones, *The Later Roman Empire*, vols. I-III, Oxford 1964;
J. Gaudemet, *L'Eglise dans l'Empire Romain*, Paris 1958.

The more notable studies of Constantine the Great include:

J. Burckhardt, *Die Zeit Konstantins des Grossen*, 1st ed. Basel 1853;
J. Maurice, *Constantine le Grand*, Paris 1924;
N. H. Baynes, *Constantine the Great and the Christian Church*, London 1929;
E. Schwartz, *Kaiser Konstantin und die christliche Kirche*, Leipzig 1936;
K. Honn, *Konstantin der Grosse*, Leipzig 1940;
A. Alföldi, *The Conversion of Constantine and Pagan Rome*, Oxford 1948;
J. Vogt, *Konstantin der Grosse*, Munchen 1948;
A. Piganiol, *L'Empereur Constantine*, Paris 1932;
A. H. M. Jones, *Constantine and the Conversion of Europe*, New York 1949;
H. Dorries, *Die Selbstzeugniss Kaisers Konstantins des Grossen*, Gottingen 1954;
H. Dorries, *Konstantin der Grosse*, Stuttgart 1958;
P. Bruun, *Studies in Constantinian Chronology*, New York 1961;
S. Calderone, *Constantino e ii cattolicesimo*, Firenze 1962.

FROM YOUR TRANSLATOR
Translating and publishing this series of books has been a labor of
love for me. I grew up reading it, and I have always wanted to be able
to share it with my American friends. And finally, here it is.
It will not make me rich, but if you liked the book, would you please
recommend it to a friend?
And if you could give it an Amazon review,
you will be helping others find it!
https://www.amazon.com/dp/B0D2V3TVL4

THANK YOU!

ABOUT THE AUTHOR

Aleksander Krawczuk (1922-2023) was a noted scholar of
Greek and Roman antiquity, a professor at the Jagiellonian
University, a former minister of culture, and an author of
over 30 popular and widely translated books on the subject
of the Antique.

ABOUT MONDRALA PRESS

Mondrala Press publishes English translations of great
Polish books—books with a track record of international
critical and commercial success but which, for political
reasons, have never been published in English.
To see our newest titles or to subscribe
to our mailing list, please visit
www.mondrala.com
THE GREATEST BOOKS YOU HAVE NEVER HEARD OF

Aleksander's Antiquities

Seven Against Thebes

Before the Trojan War, there was the Theban War. Who fought it? Why? What does archeology tell us, and what has survived of ancient the epics?

The Last Olympiad

Serapeum destroyed! Emperor murdered! Pagans raise a revolt! Read the leading lights of their time (389-395 AD) as the world as they know it ends but they debate everything from bathing to demon possession.

A Meeting in Oea

Meet Apuleius, Rome's all-time best-selling author, a Platonic scholar, a part-time magician, and a dowry-hunter, as he works on his treatise on Plato at night and schemes to marry a rich African widow by day.

Herod, King of the Jews

Herod the Great was a half-cast, a tyrant, a murderer, and he ruled by the right of conquest. But he was also the last King of the Jews to give them twenty years of peace and prosperity.

Titus and Berenice

The last vestiges of the kingdom of Judah hung for a while on the outcome of the love affair between the elderly Jewish queen Berenice, granddaughter of Herod the Great, and the 12 years younger son of Vespasian, the emperor of Rome.

Rome and Jerusalem

The end of the Jewish Trilogy: loves end, nations fall, emperors come and go.

Jacek Bocheński

Tiberius Caesar

Terror is normal.
The horrifying tale of Tiberius Caesar, the second emperor of Rome:
the man who normalized political terror. A moral, intellectual,
emotional zero whose only skill in life was to grab and hang onto
power. At any cost. A dizzying look into
the great void of an empty soul.

Joe Alex

The Ships of Minos 1-5

A Bronze Age Saga.
1600 BC. A Minoan ship sails to the ends of the world in search of the
sources of amber. Days without night, water turning to stone, monsters of
the deep, peoples who sacrifice their kings to their gods and build great
stone circles to worship the sun. And god's face upon the waters.
One of the greatest exploration sagas ever written.

Witold Makowiecki
Out of the Lion's Maw

570 B.C. They slip their jailors in Carthage and rush across the Mediterranean pursued by enemy agents and assassins: a mysterious oriental priest and his Greek apprentice. Their mission: to prevent the outbreak of a civil war in Egypt. Their opponents: the Great Phoenician Council and the entire state apparatus of Eternal Egypt. Their resources: the old man's wit and the young man's courage.

Wind from the Hospitable Sea

Greece 562 BC. For insolvent debtors, the price of bankruptcy is slavery. When his mother and siblings are seized for unpaid debts, little Diossos must run to fetch help. He must cross mountains, forests, and stormy seas, brave wild animals, slave catchers, pirates, and... the law. He has one month to achieve his quest but only days to grow up.

Arkady Fiedler

The White Jaguar 1-5

AD 1726. An uninhabited Caribbean island off the Spanish Main. A
Virginian renegade. Pirates, Runaway slaves. Cannibals.
The great saga of the mysterious White Jaguar, a white man named
John who became a war leader of the Orinoco Indians in their wars
against the Spanish.

Maria Rodziewiczówna

A Summer of the Forest Folk

The most beautiful book you will read this year.
Turn of the nineteenth century. Three women spend their summers in a remote
cottage deep in the last virgin forest in Europe. This summer, their teenage big-city
nephew joins them. A heart-warming, feel-good tale of love and friendship, of
coming of age, and of the healing power of nature. This is a book like nothing you
have ever read, a phenomenon, a genre of its own.

9 782919 820740